→ YOU CAN DO ANYTHING!

→YOU CAN DO ANYTHING!

JONNIE PEACOCK

Written in collaboration with
Laura Earnshaw

Illustrations by
Ashwin Chacko

BLOOMSBURY
CHILDREN'S BOOKS
LONDON OXFORD NEW YORK NEW DELHI SYDNEY

First published 2024 by Bloomsbury Publishing Plc
BLOOMSBURY CHILDREN'S BOOKS
Bloomsbury Publishing Plc
50 Bedford Square, London WC1B 3DP, UK
29 Earlsfort Terrace, Dublin 2, Ireland

BLOOMSBURY, BLOOMSBURY CHILDREN'S BOOKS and the Diana logo
are trademarks of Bloomsbury Publishing Plc

First published in Great Britain in 2024 by Bloomsbury Publishing Plc

ISBN: PB: 978 15266 7703 7
eBook: 978 15266 8008 2
Audio: 978 1 5266 8009 9

2 4 6 8 10 9 7 5 3 1

Printed and bound by CPI Group (UK) Ltd, Croydon CR0 4YY

MIX
Paper | Supporting
responsible forestry
FSC® C171272

To find out more about our authors and books visit
www.bloomsbury.com and sign up for our newsletters

To every single person
who strives for a better
tomorrow and breaks the
boxes we are all put in!

−J.P.

CONTENTS

BEFORE WE START

Hi, I'm **Jonnie**. Paralympic gold-medal-winning sprinter and author of this book. You'll hear **much** more about me later on, but before we get stuck in, I wanted to explain how to use my book. Before you say, 'What do you mean *HOW*? I don't want to have to *DO* anything, I just want to *READ* it' – don't panic. Basically, alongside my story and life lessons, I've packed this book full of activities called **Happiness Hacks** and **Rest Stops**. These activities link to the ideas I'll be sharing with you. You can choose to try them out, or not, it's completely up to you. Either way, let me explain a bit more about them ...

Each activity comes from either things I do already or have learned through coaches and people in my life, or from the amazing **Laura Earnshaw**, who's been collaborating with me on this book (and coined the term Happiness Hack). She is a leading expert in the science of happiness (a bit like a happiness coach) and some of these activities are **actually used** in her organisation called myHappymind (more on page 237).

One thing I've suggested is that you keep a **journal** to try out these ideas (see page 44),

That's Laura!

8

but if you don't want to do that, you can write on paper or even this book. *If you're allowed and you aren't sharing the book or borrowing it from the library!*

As you work through each chapter, I also want you to make a **plan** to keep hold of everything you've read. This is your **Race Plan** (another genius Laura idea). After each chapter, I'll ask you to summarise what you've read by filling in one lesson or 'lap'. This means that by the end of the book, you'll have a written **plan** to get you started on your **happiness journey** and sprint to the finish line – all eight laps of it. In fact, you'll be such an expert by then that you'll be able to help your friends and family fill in their own plans. After all, **sharing is caring**! I've even added a handy template with all the questions on page 222 you can either fill in or copy into your journal or onto some paper.

The other thing I'd like you to do is write down how you're feeling **RIGHT NOW**. I'll be asking you to compare how you feel before and after some of the activities, but for now, just write down how you feel **this exact moment**. You can either write it below or on a piece of paper. You could even write it on page one of your journal.

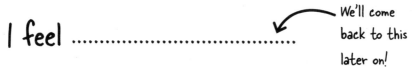

I feel .... *We'll come back to this later on!*

That's all for now. It's time to get started.

TURN THE PAGE AND LET'S GO!

THE STARTING Line

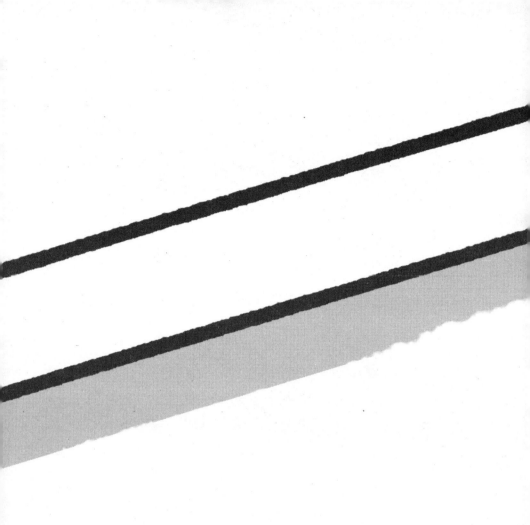

THE STARTING LINE.

This has two meanings for me. The first one is that the starting line is where I do my job as a sprinter – a job I've trained for since I was your age and absolutely love. The other is that this is the first line of my first ever book and I can't wait to get going.

Let's START!

HI THERE.

I'm Jonnie, and

I'm **happy** to meet you.

Spoiler alert: this might be a big clue for what this book is about!

YOU MIGHT HAVE PICKED UP THIS BOOK BECAUSE YOU KNOW ME, OR PERHAPS YOU JUST LIKED THE COVER. IT'S COOL, RIGHT? BUT THIS BOOK ISN'T JUST ABOUT ME. IT'S ALSO ABOUT YOU.

You might be thinking, *Hang on a second, that's YOU on the book cover, not ME!*

And yeah, you're right, that *is* me on there. I am a ballroom-dancing, dog-loving, medal-winning, record-setting Paralympic sprinter, and maybe **for now** I might be faster than you. But remember the title of the book? It's about **you**. YOU can do anything. So you're going to catch up, quickly, and you'll go far. With your body AND your brain.

When I am there at the starting line, my muscles are ready. My brain is ready. I can still notice things like the **sound** of the crowd and the **movements** of the sprinters next to me, because I'm only human (well, mostly human), and I **react**.

I think, focus and EXECUTE.

No, not execute in a scary murdering way! I shut out the noise in the stadium and in my head, and **FOCUS** on the job I am there to do ... **to run as fast as I can**. It's really the only control I have – to do the thing I have trained to do and do it in the best way **I possibly can**.

This is what I want to show you. I want to teach you how to be your own **BEST** you.

It's tricky being your age, I know. Not so long ago, I was there myself. You're trying to figure **everything** out (not just your maths homework, although that can be pretty tricky too!) and become the person you want to be. But it isn't always EASY. Some people and circumstances try to pull you down. And sometimes when you try to untangle it all, you might get a little down on yourself and feel like you're tumbling through a trapdoor. The **fear** can be unreal, and before you know it, you might knock yourself out of the race.

I DO KNOW A THING OR TWO ABOUT RACES, THOUGH. AND THEY AREN'T OVER UNTIL THEY'RE OVER. IT'S WHAT HAPPENS DURING THE RACE AND HOW YOU FACE IT – AND DEAL WITH IT – THAT COUNTS.

So how do we deal with it? You might think a little bit of **change** could solve everything. If only you were taller, faster, smarter, cooler, had more awesome hair ... you get the idea. But there is a better way to jump over life's hurdles than being someone else, and that's being the **best** and **happiest** version of yourself. Everyone can figure out what makes them **smile**. It just takes a little working out. And that's what we're going to do in this book! I'm going to **coach** you to be your best.

I say coach because that's what I know. I couldn't have got so far and definitely wouldn't be so fast without my own. But coaches aren't just for sport (although they are important if you want to be a pro like me) – **they're for life**. In this book, I'm going to try my hardest to be your coach (yes, just for you). I can show you what's worked for me, and what ideas and activities can help **you** succeed. It's just like practising your chess moves or football tricks, but this time, it's life skills – the kinds of things that shape you into the person **you really want to be**. Who knows, maybe a gold medallist?

See you at the starting line!

Listening and learning are so important, so I've got another kind of coach on board, too. That, of course, is Laura, who you met at the start of the book. She's our incredible **happiness coach** and will be at the starting line all the way through to the finish line for your sprint to your smile. *Awesome!*

I'll also share some words from people who have inspired me on my own race to be the best. I'll sprinkle in some other cool stuff, too, like how many muscles it takes to **smile** and what outside temperature is the best for being HAPPY. Yep, there really is an ideal temperature for happiness!

I'm also going to ask you try out some activities that have helped me discover what makes me happy. Get ready to pour a bucket of ice over your head – I **promise**, it'll be worth it! Plus, if you feel up for it, I'd like you to ask yourself how you're feeling every now and again and write it down. Your mood is likely to change throughout this book, so keeping track will be an interesting experiment!

It's impossible to be happy all the time, of course. It's normal to feel sad, angry or frustrated sometimes, too. But the lows only make the highs better, right?

AND DON'T FORGET, YOU REALLY CAN DO ANYTHING. THAT'S NOT JUST BECAUSE IT SAYS SO ON THE FRONT OF THE BOOK. IT'S ALL TRUE. PROMISE.

At the end, I hope you'll get to know yourself better. I really believe that this is the key to everything: **finding the true you**. Focus on your own goals, and become the very best version of yourself – whoever that may be.

You will read about me and my experiences, too, because it's my book. Obviously. But also because I hope that by sharing my story, I can help you (if I don't bore you to oblivion first!). My aim is that by the final page (all the way on page 240) you will have found plenty to think about, lots to write about, happy hacks to try, extra-resilient superpower strength and a better understanding of **who you are** and **what makes you SMILE.**

SO, WHAT ARE WE WAITING FOR ... ?

ON YOUR MARKS,

GET SET,

CHAPTER ONE

YOU ARE UNIQUE!

OH, WAIT. FALSE START!

Before you turn the page and we sprint away, I have six questions for you to think about. It's a bit like a warm-up exercise to get your brain turned on.

See if you can answer these questions as quickly as possible, then look over them and think about what you wrote. (If you're with a friend, compare your answers. I bet they won't be the same!)

Ready?

1) If you had to describe yourself in one word, what would it be?

Made-up words are allowed.

2) What is your pet peeve, or the thing that really drives you up the wall? (If you have a pet named Peeve, you can skip this one.)

3) What's the thing you like most about yourself?

Are you funny or tall? Do you have cool hair or can you jump really high?

4) If you could choose another name for yourself, what would you pick?

5) What superpower would you grant to the entire world, if you could?

6) What's something that always makes you laugh or smile so much that your face hurts?

27

YOU ARE UNIQUE!

We're beginning chapter one for real now!

Now you've answered some questions about *you*, it seems only fair I share a little bit more about *me*. I was born in Cambridge, in the UK, in 1993. I didn't live in Cambridge though. I lived on the outskirts, with my parents and three big sisters, in a little village called **Shepreth**. Would you believe one of the things the village was most famous for (before me!) was **sheep washing**? Yep, people herding sheep to Cambridge stopped in our little village to give them a bath. So, I basically grew up in a **launderette for sheep**.

Baaaa ha ha!

I was always **running, jumping** and **moving** about as a little kid. I loved to eat apples from my gran's tree, I loved learning and school, but mostly I loved football. My grandpa on Mum's side, who I never met (but was named after), was a keen player and a real **inspiration** to me. Just knowing I had someone like him in my family sparked my interest in playing football – which started me on my **sport-loving path**. My sisters taught me loads too. They were always **competitive** with me and **challenged** me to discover what I was good at (or not so good at). This included bike riding, nail painting and atomic wedgies.

Don't ask!

Then, when I was five, I got an illness called **meningitis**, which is when the lining around your brain and spinal column gets infected and acts up **big time**. After being put into a coma, the doctors managed to get the meningitis under control (phew), but complications from the illness led to a load of pressure building up in my leg (uh-oh). I won't bore you with all the medical details, but this meant the doctors had to amputate my leg to save my life.

NOT fun!

It was really tough to begin with. For starters, I had to learn to walk all over again. To run, jump, move and play football **all over again**. It was also tricky because, as you know, when you're a kid you just want to be the same as everyone else. And now I was **different**. But luckily for me, I had the most **amazing** support and I worked hard to get to grips with my new leg. Finally, after a while, I **learned** to cope.

TO JUST DO WHAT I COULD DO AND EVENTUALLY COME OUT THRIVING. TO WALK AGAIN SO I COULD RUN.

And speaking of thriving, my journey eventually led me to **sprinting** (more about that later). Turns out the art of running really fast is what propels me (literally and figuratively) forwards. By finding what makes me, **me**, I went on to win **Paralympic**, **World** and **European** sprint titles and I am still running, still believing. Still **smiling**. And I never knew this life was possible.

Of course I know not everyone will become a Paralympic champion. But everyone **can** find what makes them smile. Be it horse riding or DJing. Which brings me back to you – because what did I tell you about this book? **It's about YOU**! So, let me hit you with a big idea, one of the most **important ideas** I want to show you about yourself. Hopefully it's something you've noticed from the questions I asked you earlier, or from reading my own **one-of-a-kind story**. But here goes …

... YOU ARE ABSOLUTELY, TOTALLY, 100 PER CENT UNIQUE!

Give them back! ⟋

He really needs that! ⟍

You might have your mum's eyes or your dad's hair, but you are **completely one of a kind**. You, me, your friends, teachers, parents, dog and stick insect are like **no one else**.

But what does that mean in numbers? Well, there are 8.1 billion people on Earth today. It's pretty impossible to imagine a number that size, so imagine this. Think of a big stadium like London's Olympic Stadium. Say every single one of those 80,000 seats is filled and the crowd is going bonkers, perhaps for the appearance of a young amazing Paralympic sprinting superstar? (Sound like anyone you know?) Then imagine each of those seats is its own Olympic stadium, also **filled to the max**. That works out at 80,000 times 80,000. Add another 1.7 <u>billion</u> people and that's how many people there are in the world. And counting!

That's going to be one long line for the loo.

STILL, AMONG ALL THOSE PEOPLE, THERE IS JUST ONE YOU.

> ## *"Maybe you're not meant to fit in. Maybe you're supposed to stand out."*
> – Taylor Swift

FAST FACT:

If your name happens to be Muhammad, there are at least **150 million** other people in the world who have the same name as you. But what's cool is that each Muhammad is still different from the next. You are, and will always be, your own unique Muhammad.

What does unique mean? Well, if you ask a dictionary, it will say that being unique is **being one of a kind**. Unlike anything or anyone else.

The French created the word 'unique' by borrowing from the **Latin** word *unicus*, which means 'the only one'. (Like a unicorn = one horn, or unicycle = one wheel.)

FAST FACT:
At least 60 per cent of all English words have Latin roots. This ancient language has given us many words we still use today, like *ad infinitum* (which means 'doing the same thing over and over again forever') and *vice versa* ('the other way around')!

Some people think being called unique is an **insult**. Kind of like saying someone is weird, strange or doesn't belong. Someone who needs to change. But that's not right. Think of the **unicorn**, or the unicycle. Or think of me. If I'd been just like everyone else, I wouldn't have had the life I've had. And how **rubbish** would that have been?

You see the world in your own way, even if you don't think about it that much. You have your own opinions, ideas and thoughts. **You were born to be you**. And you know what? The world needs different thinkers to progress. Think about Albert Einstein – he had his own opinions, ideas and thoughts and he **changed the world with them**.

All the experiences you've had, the things you like and dislike, your personality, the ways you communicate, your interactions with family and friends and so many other things, down to what you eat for breakfast, have made you **what you are**.

Eggs, please!

REST STOP

Always be yourself

Make a list of five things that are unique to you. You can use really small handwriting or a secret code if you don't want anyone to see. This could be anything from the mole on your pinky finger to your favourite book or the way you pronounce certain words.

But how do you know if all of those things you wrote down are **REALLY** unique to you? There might be someone on the other side of the world with a mole in the exact same spot. Or a few million people with the same favourite colour as you. Well, there's one thing that makes you really, truly, one-of-a-kind unique. Can you guess what it is? The answer is right at your **fingertips** ...

FINGERPRINTS!

If you're lacking limbs like me and don't have fingers, look at a friend's or family member's.

Look at the tips of your fingers. Do you see those little scrunchy, squirmy, wiggly lines snaking around on them? When you touch things, the oil and dirt on your hands leave behind **marks** we know as **fingerprints**. The patterns on those fingerprints come from those little squiggly lines.

This is weird, but these fingerprints were formed **before** you were born. When you were just hanging out in your mum's tummy. Even stranger, no one else in those multiple stadiums we spoke about

earlier has the **exact same prints** as you. Literally NO ONE. What's even STRANGER is that those funny prints can be used to catch bad guys.

Cool.

And do you know what else is a bit like your fingerprints? Your **brain**! Yes, it's squishy and covered in squiggly lines – but it is one of a kind too. With its own unique thoughts, feelings and opinions. I want you to think about that every time you look at yours or someone else's fingerprints. Think of your brain, and how it's like **no one else's**. Does it get much cooler than that?

FAST FACT:

Koalas have very similar prints to humans. So, if you decided to commit a crime, the FIRST crime you should commit is borrowing a koala from the zoo and letting it leave its fingerprints at the crime scene, instead of you. Genius!

See how much you have learned already, and it's only chapter one?

REST STOP

Your unique brain

I like to think of my fingerprints as outward representations of my brain. They are unique to us, just like that lump of goo between our ears that makes us who we are. Combined with toe prints, palm prints, lip prints, elbow prints, ear prints and stump prints, you're as one of a kind as can be. (That's right, if you don't have any of those body parts, chances are you have a stump, which has its own unique print).

To make your own outward representation of your brain, I want you to use some ink, paint or melted chocolate and put your different prints on this page or in your journal (more about that on page 44). Ask your friends to share their prints too or ask them if you can see their fingerprints if you're missing a limb like me.

Take a look at the different prints. Compare yours and your friends. What do you notice? What does that tell you about you and your friends' brains? You might need a magnifying glass for this one!

Why am I telling you all of this? It's because I want you to **remember** that you are you, and you are **the only you**. From your fingerprints to you brain. But the thing is, lots of times the world would prefer you to change. To come out of your lane and merge with everyone else's. This can sometimes feel good – so you don't stand out too much. But, as a sprinter, if I left my lane I'd crash into someone and get disqualified. The same goes for you.

> *"To be yourself in a world that is constantly trying to make you something else is the greatest accomplishment."*
> – Ralph Waldo Emerson

You put the 'u' in 'unique'. I hope you're starting to **believe** me. Here's the thing: I was a kid once. When I was in school, I really did not want to be unique. I wanted to dress the same way, talk the same way, like the same things, act the same way as everyone else. You know what I mean. You don't want to stand out like a sore thumb, no matter if it has its own individual thumbprint. You want to fit in. You want to be liked.

Dan the Man

My first coach, Dan Pfaff, had a brilliant approach to almost everything. He told me not to worry about things I cannot change. Just worry about what's happening in my lane. OK, you might not work in a lane like I do, but you get the idea. Relax and see what happens. Don't change because you think it'll make something easier. A thousand things could happen, and not all of them are going to be the 'Worst Thing Ever'. Some of them might even be the 'Best Thing Ever'.

Happiness Hack

Happy in your skin

Think about someone you love and why you love them. Now think about something that is 100 per cent unique to them. (Don't say fingerprints! That's too easy.) Ask yourself whether you would want that person to change to match everyone else? I doubt it.

Now apply that to the things you might want to change about yourself.

Would you really want to change the bits about you that make you you, even if it makes life easier sometimes? Or do you want to be you, the truest version of you, and just be happy in your own skin?

> **"Always be yourself, express yourself, have faith in yourself, do not go out and look for a successful personality and duplicate it."**
> – Bruce Lee

The problem is, it's **impossible** to fit in with everybody. Remember all those people filling 80,000 sports stadiums? Everyone with their own likes, ideas, thoughts and even insecurities?

We are not meant to be the same. We can't force people to like us or agree with us or understand us. Or even be at all interested in us! **It's way better to get to know and to like yourself**.

Shake hands with yourself (and your or your friend's fingerprints) and say, 'This is me. I am unique. I don't need to change myself. I only need to understand myself as best I can, and **run on my own track**.'

BEING ONE OF A KIND CAN BE FUN! AND WHETHER YOU STAY THAT WAY OR NOT IS UP TO YOU.

I didn't always feel happy about being different, but now every time I get to the finish line I think, *I want to do that again. I love what I do. I'm glad I'm me.* And the more you **understand** about yourself, the less you are going to be like everyone else. And the more you're going to smile.

So here's how we're going to capture your own story. Let's start by **opening the book of you** ...

Write it out

There is one cool way to learn about who you
are and what makes you unique: start a journal.

Yes, I know you already have one book in your
hand, but think of this as a Buy One, Get One
Free sort of offer. I am encouraging you to
create your own book that you can look back on.
One where you are the author. You can use it as
you read through this book. And it will be all
yours … you might even say it'll be unique.

What to do:

1. Get yourself a notebook. Any notebook will do.
It can be big or teeny tiny. It just depends what
YOU like best.

2. Find yourself a pen or pencil — anything you
can write with. You can use pink ink, black ink
or glow-in-the-dark ink — it's completely up
to you.

I like using a pencil so I can rub out any spelling mistakes!

3. Go wild designing the cover! You can draw on it, put stickers on it, use markers or add graffiti. You could even add your fingerprints! Whatever you fancy. It's your book and you can do what you want with it.

4. The book you create is going to be your friend, so you need to give it a name. I once had a diary called my 'Paralympics Diary'.

Can you guess when I wrote it?

Here are some journal name ideas to get you started:

- The Big Brilliant Book of Me

- You Can Do Anything

Sorry, already taken!

- Hands off!

Even cooler if you also add your handprint to the front!

- The Koala Did It, Not Me

- Jonnie Peacock Told Me to Make This

Now you've got what you need to make a journal, here's how I think this could work. Throughout this book, I'll give you some starters to get you ... erm, started. Ideas, activities, questions, moments to reflect. All sorts. Try to write those bits down in your journal. But remember – these are just **starters**. You can write anything in your journal you want. You also don't need a journal if you'd prefer to scribble in this book instead.

I'm only going to say this one more time but DO NOT write in this book if it's a library book or you're sharing it with someone else!

Expressing yourself in a journal is pretty **cool**. It's a great way to understand yourself and communicate your thoughts. It's also a good way of finding out what has been making you **happy** or **sad. Question yourself!** Scribble and doodle away! You never know what you might find out. Why? Because ...

... YOU CAN DO ANYTHING!

RACE PLAN: *LAP ONE*

Your best bits

Write down three things you like about yourself. Then write down what the people in the list below might say are your three strengths:

- A teacher
- A grown-up in your life
- A friend
- That pigeon who's been staring at you

Ok, maybe not the pigeon.

Hold on to those words. Write them down in sparkly gel pen and underline them. Come back to those words whenever you feel like the world is trying to make you be someone different.

You can use this space for any notes you want to
make about what you've learnt in this chapter!

CHAPTER TWO

FIND WHAT YOU LOVE!

Me again. Now you know you're totally, 100 per cent unique, we're going to open things up a little bit so that we can begin to find out more about **the true you**. This does not involve opening your stinky sock drawer. It's about finding the things that **stop the world** for you. That make you smile. The things you **love** doing. Just like I love massive burgers, fast cars and video games. ← *And running really, really fast, of course!*

When I'm playing a video game, I go into an autopilot world, where **nothing else** matters but the 'now'.

That's really important to me. Shutting out the rest of the world so I can breathe. I get that feeling when I run, too. Or when I **finish** a race. Even when I take my dogs, Luna and Bella, for a walk.

I love my **lucky charms**, the items I carry on races, for the same reason. I always have a **St Christopher** charm and an **army badge** that my grandpa wore on me when I run an important race. Either in a pocket or, when I don't have one of those, I tape them to my leg. They make me feel **calm**. (Except that time I dropped them out of my waistband and had reporters and fellow athletes looking all over the track for them! Luckily, they were handed in to lost property. Phew!)

FAST FACT:
Previous Women's World Marathon Record-Holder Paula Radcliffe has her own lucky charm. She uses the same safety pins to attach her running number to her vest for every race.

What I'm trying to say is, it's good to find out what you **love**. What makes you feel **good**, **calm**, **safe** and **happy**. The best way to start doing that is to learn to read your **mind** ... Bear with me on this one.

You are, at present, reading a book. Now what if I convinced you that you could read yourself like a book? Sounds silly, but trust me. Anyone can learn to do it and it's a great way to check in with yourself so you can **take care of yourself**. Especially with all those thoughts **swirling** around in your head.

REST STOP

How do you feel?

Before we get fully into 'reading' yourself, I want you to stop and pay attention to your mood and your body. Ask yourself these questions:

- How do I feel right now? Do I feel happy, sad, relaxed, confused, excited, calm, angry?
- What is my body doing right now? Am I sitting cross-legged, are my arms crossed, am I slumped over or sitting up straight?
- What is my face doing? If I were to get a camera or a mirror right now without changing my expression, what would it tell me about my mood?

Now I want you to do something you love. That you enjoy. This can be eating your favourite snack, taking a long bath ← *Don't drop your book in it though!* or speaking to a friend. Then ask yourself the same questions you did before. Are the answers different?

You might imagine that I've become a **Mysterious Moustachioed Magician** in a cape, 'reading' your mind while trying to stuff a squirmy rabbit into a top hat for my next trick. Even though sometimes I do have a moustache, this isn't *quite* what I mean.

What I mean is, there aren't any magic tricks to get through life. ⟵ Unfortunately.
There's no magic spell to peer through your ears, into your brain and find the **answers** (not even the fingerprint trick can do that). Magic tricks are just that, magic. And (as much as it pains me to say it) magic

↗ Possibly because of all the earwax.

isn't real. As much as I'd like to say all you need is a magic spell and you'll find out who you are and what makes you **happy**, I can't. It's about **learning** and **understanding** yourself, and being very kind to that magic rabbit (aka, your brain). And it takes a bit of work.

What you have to learn and practise is something called **mindfulness**. You might have heard of this or you might not have, but even if you know what it is, let me tell you a bit more about it because I think it's **really cool**.

Mindfulness is something you can do to make yourself aware of your **body**, **mind** and **feelings**. Where you only think about the moment you're in – like when I'm playing Xbox or walking my dogs. It's just a chance to say hello to your brain and try to get those busy thoughts to leave you alone for a minute.

I try to channel that feeling when I'm standing on the starting block. I could be thinking, *AAAAARGH! How am I going to do this? I really, REALLY want to win! What about the guy next to me? He looks super fast. What if I mess up? How can I be better, faster? What time is it? Are my laces tied? Are my lucky charms securely fastened?*

I definitely *could* be thinking all those things. But what I try to do instead is be **mindful**. I try not to let my brain fill up. I calm those thoughts down so I can do what I do best – **run**. So that's what I want you to do.

CALM THE NOISE SO YOU CAN RUN.

Think about everything that's in your brain, every second, every minute, every day. It's like a **cacophony** in there.

Now, that's a big word. A cacophony is a loud mix of sounds that **clash** and **clang** – a bit like all the noisy thoughts banging around in your brain. Now think about all those thoughts. *What day is it? Did I remember my homework? What was it I promised Mum I'd do? Do I smell funny? Am I having potatoes for tea tonight? Do I even like potatoes? Am I even hungry?*

Stuffed in there with all the thoughts are **feelings** and **sensations** too, coming at you from all over the place. The way the sun warms your face, how your toes squiggle around in the grass, the sound of the bus you just missed, the way your skin stretches when you smile, the way you feel when you spot your mates, the memory of something that makes you feel calm. There are no doubt some **worries** and **scary feelings** in the mix, too. But that's OK. Life is like that.

FAST FACT:

Some brainy people have guessed that humans have around 6,000 thoughts a day while we're awake. It can feel like we have 600 million sometimes though.

So, your brain is pretty full up, all the time. Mind-**full**, *I couldn't resist!* get it? It's a wonder our heads are not ten times the size to fit that all in. If they were, you might look a little like a potato-head toy and have serious trouble finding a bike helmet.

Being mindful means pausing for a moment. Just like pressing **pause** on a YouTube video or on Netflix. Though I am not talking about pausing on clips of me winning races or *paws*-ing on videos of cute dogs. *Too easy!*

It's a moment to slooooooow down. (And this is from a sprinter who goes faaaaaaaast!) Take time to **listen** to your potato head or rabbit brain. ← Ha ha!

Concentrate on just one **thought** or **feeling** at a time. It's not calming down, exactly. It's just **listening** to what you are experiencing at this very moment in time. Understand what's going on, even if the chips are down.

Potato joke – sorry!

Once you understand the ideas behind **checking in with yourself**, **reading yourself** and **understanding yourself** – you can use those tools to figure out the things that make you **happy**. The things that make you, **you**. You'll learn loads of tips throughout the book on how to be mindful too (that thing I mentioned just a few pages ago) but don't worry too much about that for now. Just try your best to engage with the activities in this book. If you do, you'll come to understand this idea without even realising it. And that's when the magic **really** starts to kick in.

Speaking of magic, let's talk about the **science** of **you**. Because you know I said magic isn't real? That's not technically true. Your body is magic because it can do **so much**. Want to know more?

You're atomic, made up of **atoms**. That's the smallest part of a **chemical element** that can exist. Everything in the universe is built with these teeny, tiny things. How many atoms are there stuffed inside the average person? Around seven billion billion billion. That's a seven followed by 27 zeroes, and some commas thrown in there, too.

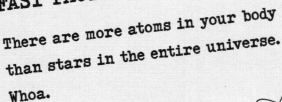

FAST FACT:

There are more atoms in your body than stars in the entire universe. Whoa.

Your body has some mostly solid stuff: a skeleton, muscles, skin, your hairdo, etc. It's also got liquid stuff, like water, blood and ooze. All of it, though, is made from **atoms**, which make up your body cells. So many cells! Your brain alone has at least **171 billion** of them rattling around.

And remember, you are unique!

If there were a **recipe** for you, you'd need to mix up a whole lot of oxygen atoms, some carbon, hydrogen and nitrogen, plus a pinch or two of other small, but important elements. Like clean **underpants**. And maybe a nice **hat**.

Where am I going with this? Good question. I want you to start thinking about how, from these super-small building blocks that we all share, you've become you. I want you to realise that your body, and all the bits in it, aren't **separate** from your thoughts and feelings. It's all **connected**. And you can even hack your thoughts and feelings by being active or standing in a cold shower. Don't panic! I'll tell you more about that in chapter four.

So here you are, sloshing around with all those atoms, the same ones everyone has. Plus all those **feelings** and **sensations**. And, of course, that nice hat you're wearing. And you might be wondering – what is it that makes me **special**?

A huge part of what makes you special is finding out what you **love**. The things that never fail to make you **happy**. I call this '**The Happiness Question**'.
But do you **really** know the things you enjoy, the stuff that makes you calm and what you're pretty good at?

Some of those might be stuff you love to do with your **mates**. Other things might be what you love to do by **yourself**. I think of it as the stuff that helps me **calm down**, takes my mind off any worries and leaves me with a **smile on my face**.

Happiness Hack

Just think it

Close your eyes and think about one thing that you really enjoy doing. It could be anything: stroking your dog, playing a video game or hanging out with your siblings. Whatever pops into your head. Now try and imagine doing it in as much detail as possible and sit with that thought for a moment. Then open your eyes and see how you feel. Compare this to how you felt before doing it.

I'll be honest with you. I didn't always know the answer to **The Happiness Question** myself. One thing I really wanted to do when I was a kid was **draw**. Drawing seemed like a really incredible and cool way to **express** yourself. I wanted to be so good at it, like **Jonnie Picasso Peacock**. BUT! One of my mates was already an **expert**.

Which was drawing the wrong conclusion!

He was so good, that I just gave up. I thought I'd always look rubbish next to him. And since I'd never be able to do what he could do, I thought, why even try? So I took the easy way out and quit. But you know what? **I really wish I hadn't**. Think of all the fun I have missed out on by not even trying? And by now, surely I'd be pretty **good**. Maybe not quite up to my amazing illustrator Ashwin's level, but close.

Running away from a challenge, right?

I confess: I even felt like quitting sprinting at first. I didn't think I'd ever be good enough. But if something makes you feel good, you shouldn't run away from it. And this time I'm so glad I didn't. I stuck to it and I got a lot better. I kept going.

We are all unique, and we can bring that to anything that will make us **happy**. But how do we find those unique things?

Especially if you do not live near an ocean.

Everyone has a special **purpose**. I prefer to think of it as a **porpoise**. Finding that porpoise can be really tough and frustrating. You might be really good at something (or lots of things) right now, but where do you want that to **take you**?

REST STOP

Discovering your porpoise

I want to come back to that journal idea I was talking about on page 44. Keeping a journal and writing with love, care and affection about yourself can really boost your well-being and help you learn about yourself. What you write need not be about what you did every day, but can be about wonderful experiences and people in your life, what you imagine your future to be, what went really well for you in the last few days, what kind of things you like to do that give you a sense of porpoise.

OK, you might not exactly know your porpoise yet, but you could realise you want to be around animals.

Just writing something down every day, or every few days, can help you understand yourself and help you find your porpoise, too.

70

SHOUT OUT!

Brilliant Becks

When I was seven, I met my hero: football superstar David Beckham. It was just two years after I lost my leg and it was a complete dream come true to meet him. He signed a training top for me that I still have today. I often think of that being what made me such a sport-lover. Perhaps if I'd never met David, I'd never have found my porpoise?

So, if something catches your **attention**, or your **porpoise**, just give it a go! Throw yourself in. You'll never know if you don't try. And if you're already doing something that brings you **joy**, keep doing it.

Sure, it might take some time to learn what you really love and some stuff won't work out for you. But you know what? I've learned so much more from my losses than my wins. So don't be afraid of it not working out. Just **trying** can put a smile on your face, happiness in your pocket and a porpoise in your bathtub (maybe). **Anything is possible, as long as you want it.**

I asked you not to look in the sock drawer, thank you.

Finding your dream is not easy. But **everyone** can figure out the things that bring them joy. Don't feel worried about it. If you don't enjoy something, or feel pressured to enjoy it, try to move on!

Unless it's your maths homework!

You'll soon find the special thing that has **your name** all over it.

Plan your dream day

Imagine if you could have a day filled with everything you love. Make a plan for how your perfect day would go. What would you do each step of the day? What time would you get up and what time would you go to bed? What would you eat? Who would you see, or not see?

Why not draw a poster imagining your dream day too. You could even show it to friends or family if you felt brave enough!

RACE PLAN: *LAP TWO*

Finding joy

Find five things that bring you joy. Things that you love doing. That leave you feeling refreshed, happy, energised or calm.

Try not to let your thoughts be influenced by your friends or family. Try to make sure they're specific to you. Then write them down.

Here are some prompts to help you:

- What do you want to spend more time doing, and what don't you enjoy so much?

- What makes you feel calm or takes your mind off your worries?

- What are you good at or want to be better at?

- What do you enjoy doing with friends and enjoy doing on your own?

- Do you do anything at the moment that you don't enjoy or that you feel pressured to enjoy? Why don't you like it?

You can use this space for any notes you want to make about what you've learnt in this chapter!

CHAPTER THREE

MAKE IT HAPPEN!

Now you know how to **read your mind**, you've hopefully started to think about what it is that you **love**. The sports, activities, games, hobbies, interests and lessons that make you SMILE. These might include criminal koalas, pointy porpoises, mind-reading magicians or running really, really fast – the possibilities are **endless**.

But how do you build on what you love and aim to **keep** those things in your life? Or change and **grow** into new things you might not even **know** you love yet?

All of us have probably been asked, 'What do you want to be when you grow up?' But instead of saying, 'Errr ... taller', let's **really** think about that **question**. And the **answers**.

For this to work, we need to open up your brain. No, we're not about to start performing brain surgery. Though perhaps if you like the sound of that, you should add 'become a brain surgeon' to your answers for 'What do I want to be when I grow up?'.

But I'm getting side-tracked. I want you to open up your brain in a slightly different way. I want to introduce you to someone.

PLEASE
MEET ...

I find that thinking about the Future Jonnie helps me focus on what Present Jonnie wants or needs. By channelling what it is that I **imagine** for myself, I can start to **understand** what is important now, without even realising it. In order to try this for yourself, you need to do some **dreaming**.

Here's the 'brain opening' I was talking about!

I want you to think about **Future You**. That could be you in two weeks, two months, two years or two decades! It doesn't matter when, it just matters that this is a **you** in the **future**. Now imagine the world you want to live in, how you might shape it, what you want to do, what you're good at and the kind of person you want to be. Is Future You wearing a **suit** or a **tracksuit**? Are they trekking through the **jungle** or inputting top-secret data into a **computer**? Are they **helping** people or **asking** for help?

It can be quite hard to get into this way of thinking, so let's start by doing a dump. No, not *that* kind of dump (though it is a bit like that). A **brain dump**. Aka dumping your thoughts out without thinking too much about them! You can write these thoughts and ideas down in your journal or at the end of this chapter, draw a picture, make a collage or even build a sand sculpture ... do it in whatever way feels **right** for you. You just have to get the ideas out of your head into something you can take inspiration from. Conjure up everything that comes to mind when you think about what you love and what your **dreams** and **wishes** are for the future.

YOU DON'T NEED TO THINK TOO MUCH ABOUT IT, OR GET DOWN IN THE DUMPS, JUST DUMP!

Predicting the future

Write down three things you love. Then write down a job or future persona that links to that thing. For example:

I LOVE: <u>Running</u>

=

Easy!

FUTURE ME:
— <u>Paralympic Gold Medal Winner</u>

This type of thinking applies to what you **DON'T** want for Future You too. The Future Not You. If you can't imagine what Future You is doing, think about what Future You is <u>not</u> doing. You can then look over what you put down, and use it to help you understand what it is you **DO** want.

I just want you to dream as big as you can. Be as **daring**, **bold** and **brilliant** as possible with your imagination. Remember, it's *your* imagination.

Sorry, another sprinter joke!

There are *literally* no limits! Don't get stuck at the starting block thinking about the 'how', just run with it and have fun. **DREAM BIG! BECAUSE IF YOU THINK SMALL, YOU'LL STAY SMALL.**

You've heard that saying, **think outside of the box**, right? That doesn't mean you have to crawl in and out of a box to think, unless that sounds fun to you. It's more a way to question what you are **expected** to say or do. For instance, I'm often thought of as being 'less able' because I have a disability. But you know what? I'm actually **more able** than 90 per cent of people. If you were to put an obstacle course in front of me and a selection of random people, I'd likely win. So my way of thinking outside the box is **challenging those perceptions** and doing what I love anyway. And to think, my 100-metre sprint record is only 1.06 seconds away from world record breaker Usain Bolt.

FAST FACT:

At the US Paralympic Track & Field Trials in 2012, I broke the single leg amputee world record for the 100-metre sprint, with a time of 10.85 seconds.

Lightning Bolt

This man needs no introduction. Seriously. I'm actually kind of racking my brains to think of something I can say about the icon that is Usain Bolt. Well – he's the fastest man in the world, that seems like a good start. And he's another hero of mine. He's a guy who thought about his future self, and went and found him — training relentlessly, setting himself targets and striving to just get a little bit better each and every time he ran. He famously said: "If you want to be the best, or you want to strive for more, you've got to set goals in life." And if Usain Bolt tells you that's what you should do, you know it's good advice. So let's set some goals and meet Future You.

That's all to say, just cut out the **noise** and **channel** what I taught you in chapter two. Grasp what it is that you love and makes you feel good, then let your **imagination**, **curiosity**, **feelings** and **sense of wonder** go wild. This kind of out-of-the-box thinking will help you understand yourself more. And the more you do it, the more you'll understand. I recommend trying to do this once every few weeks or, if that's too tricky, every few months.

REST STOP

Drawing future you

Why not try drawing a picture of Future You? (Or Future Not You.) You can imagine what you might be wearing or doing in the picture. What job, haircut or home does this person have? Just have fun with it and see where you go. Then, if you're feeling brave, you could show this to a grown-up and see what they think about it.

RED BLUE

By doing this, I hope it will help you conjure up all kinds of **Possible Yous**. ← *Future You's cousins.*

They don't all have to be the same. One can be a **builder**, the other a **fashion designer**. One might like playing **hockey**, the other **making music**. It's just about trying to channel the future in the way you see it. By doing this, you're not just stretching your imagination, but stretching the possibilities that lie ahead of you.

> *"Never set limits, go after your dreams, don't be afraid to push the boundaries. And laugh a lot – it's good for you!"*
> **– Paula Radcliffe**

IF YOU CAN SEE IT — WHO SAYS YOU CAN'T BE IT?

My entire career started by doing this, I just didn't realise it at the time.

When I was 15, I went for a check-up at the prosthetics centre in Cambridge. As you might imagine, I spent a lot of time bored out of my brain in hospital waiting rooms. Hours and hours of sitting around. The silver lining? I got really good at wheelchair wheelies. But one day, mid-wheelie, something **caught my eye**. In fact, it seemed to have been placed on the wall just for sports-loving me: a poster asking if you were aged 14 to 30 (tick) and keen on sports (double tick).

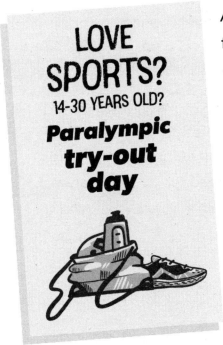

After all that ticking (and a few more wheelies) I saw my consultant and asked her about the poster. She told me there was a **Paralympic try-out day** coming up in London. Participants could have a go at all kinds of different sports, while talent-spotters kept a lookout for likely contenders. Her words were music to my ears! I knew in that moment I **had** to go to London and give it a go. The only problem? The try-outs took place on a school day.

Luckily, my mum let me have the day off school for it and she and my stepdad took me down to London. **GET IN!** When I got there it was like a **playground** for me. I had so much fun trying all the cool sports, from **shooting** to **wheelchair tennis**. Despite my wheelie skills, I found wheelchair tennis was *not* for me. I wanted to use my leg as well as my arms. So I kept trying more and more different sports. Things I never even knew existed, let alone that I could compete in. It was a brilliant day of pushing the limits of what I thought I was capable of. Finally I landed on one box that had my name all over it: the **athletics zone**.

I gave it my all and sprinted like I was being chased by a ferocious lion (or thieving koala). I felt so free! It was just incredible. That, and meeting so many other **amputees**. I felt like I belonged. No matter what was going to happen, that feeling stuck with me. I was thinking out of the box, and running away from boxes that could hold me back.

After that, I imagined myself **winning medals**, and running for my country at the **Paralympics**. Then I imagined I might even **win**. By picturing it, I worked hard to make it happen. And I couldn't be **happier** I did. Little did I know that Future Me would appear to me while I was bored in a hospital waiting room, but **I'm so glad he did**. Your Future You might appear to you when you least expect it too. But listen to them when they show up – who knows where they might take you?

That's all to say that here's my advice for you: after you've dumped your brain out, make some **plans**. Set some **goals**. Just like I did without even realising it. I set a goal to go to the try-outs, then to practise, finally to winning a Paralympic gold medal. I cringe when I hear that old cliché, **if you fail to plan, you plan to fail**. But it's true, really. If a little bit annoying.

Happiness Hack

Goal setting

Once you've thought about WHO Future You is, think about the HOW and WHY behind this conjured-up creation. 'WHO is the person I aspire to be?', 'WHY do I like this person?' and 'HOW am I going to make it so I can become this person?'. One way to achieve the HOW is to make a plan by setting <u>goals</u>:

Step 1. Make sure your goal is clear (what are you aiming for?), safe (will my goal hurt me or anyone else?) and comes from the right place (am I doing this for me or because a friend or someone else told me to?).

Step 2. Describe what success will look like – how will you know when you have achieved your goal?

Step 3. What steps do you need to take to get to your goal – what are the obstacles standing in your way? What do you actually need to do to get there?

Step 4. Identify what help you might need. Who can you speak to so you can get that help? Or what books or websites could you use to find answers?

Once you've done all of that, it's just a case of putting it all into action. Easy!

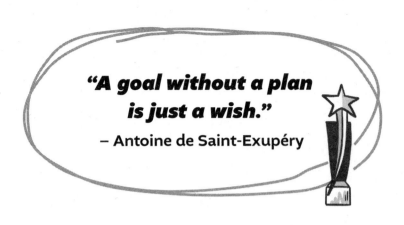

> **"A goal without a plan
> is just a wish."**
>
> – Antoine de Saint-Exupéry

Let's talk more about planning your **goals**. With your planning, you can start **small**. In sprinting, either you're first across the line, or you aren't – there's no guessing who won. I like that. But life is not quite that **simple**. Yet little steps can get you across your own finish line. They give you realistic **missions** that you can celebrate achieving.

Because there's nothing better hitting your goals!

And when it gets tough, you can push yourself to keep going by using what I like to call my '**sprints**'. These 'sprints' are like mini motivational mantras that encourage me to push through adversity and keep doing what I need to do to reach my goals.

My sprints could be: *I will give this a proper go. I will aim to get better at whatever I try. I will focus on the gain and not the pain. I won't give up unless that seems like the right thing to do for me. I will listen to myself even if THAT is a bit annoying, too.*

None of your missions needs to be **impossible**. Did I think on that first day of running around the track I'd be running in the Paralympics? No. But I told myself I could learn to run **better**, **faster**, **harder** – and I did. Likewise, I wasn't a big reader and struggled with creative writing at school, but I knew I wanted to make a book **to help kids like you**. Did I tell myself, 'No way, Jonnie. You can't do that'? Or did I go and find myself someone who could help me make the book I wished I had when I was your age? Well, you're the one reading the book, so you tell me.

The important thing was, for all of this, I didn't think I couldn't. Hey, wait! That English teacher who was trying to get me into creative writing said not to use double negative words in a sentence. So instead of, 'I didn't think I couldn't', that should be, 'I <u>DID</u> THINK I <u>COULD</u>' – and that's so **true**.

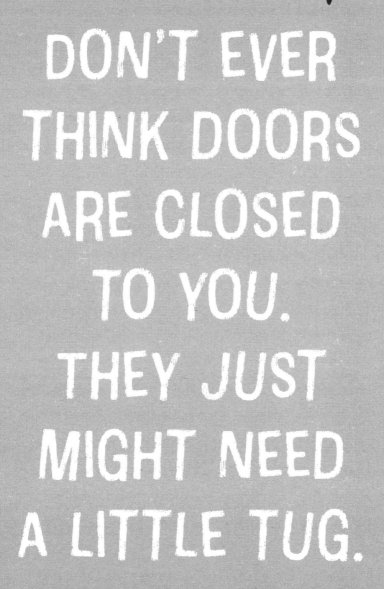

DON'T EVER
THINK DOORS
ARE CLOSED
TO YOU.
THEY JUST
MIGHT NEED
A LITTLE TUG.

Happiness coach Laura says **you can't achieve your goals if you can't define them**. So, let's look back at that brain dump you did on page 81. What did you wish for? If you knew there was no chance you would mess up and there were no obstacles standing in your way, what would you really, really want to do?

Make that your **BIG, GINORMOUS** goal. Then split it down into smaller goals. For example, I wanted to be a sprinter, so my first steps (ha ha) were learning to run on a blade, making sure I had a blade that fit, training and training more, finding a great coach, practising and practising more, eating the right food, building muscle and brain strength, and fitting training into my daily routine.

I wanted to write a book, so I wrote down some ideas, did some research, spoke to a literary agent who helped me find a publisher, who then helped me get my words onto a page and into your hands.

It's so much easier to take **small steps** to a **big goal**. You can also celebrate every step of the way to keep you going. I know that's what I do.

Pizza party, anyone? —

KNOCK, KNOCK. WHO'S THERE? OPPORTUNITY. AND WHO'S ANSWERING? IT'S YOU!

YOU are in charge. You can think about where you want to be, and work out how to get there. It's like a **map** for your **brain**. It's not going to be easy. You might have to stop for **directions**. There might be roadworks on your **journey**. Or koala poo. But if you choose it, you can do it.

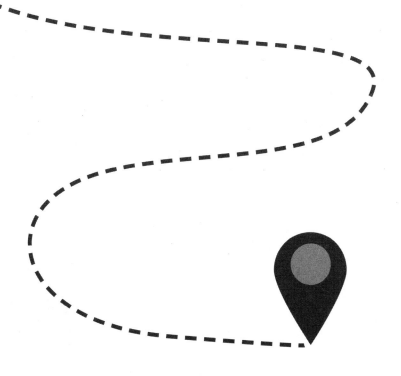

Let's celebrate!

Once you know what you want to achieve and you've broken it down into manageable goals, all you need to do is hit those goals. It's a great achievement to make something happen like that – so I like to celebrate whenever I reach a goal. Why not think of fun ways you can celebrate hitting your own goals? Here are some ideas:

- Throw a party for family, friends or your dog
- Make a hat with 'I reached my goal' on it and wear it for the day
- Give yourself an evening or day off from hitting goals to relax – you could spend this time reading, writing, playing games, watching TV, making music – whatever makes you feel good
- Eat a bowl of ice cream
- Play a board game with friends
- Go to the cinema
- Bake a cake

How will you celebrate?

To help you break it down, you can use this chart. Either fill it in here or copy it into your journal:

What do I want to achieve?	How will I get there? What are my manageable goals?	How will I celebrate each goal?

RACE PLAN: *LAP THREE*

Goal setting

Write down your three top goals. Why not pick one easy-peasy one, one slightly harder one and one that will take a bit more work. What will you be doing to celebrate when you achieve them?

You can use this space for any notes you want to make about what you've learnt in this chapter!

CHAPTER FOUR

YOU ARE ELECTRIC!

OK, we've had a bit of a brain dump. Now, let's talk about the important ways your brain **connects** with your body.

Yuck, don't step in any squishy brain bits as we move along!

Everybody has a body, right? Even if it is missing a bit like mine. And everybody has a mind. And most of the time, they work together brilliantly so that you tick along nicely. But sometimes, there's a **gap** between them. It may feel easier sometimes to let your body and your brain just **ignore** each other.

Say you have a big exam coming up at school. Your mind might think you should stay up super late and cram that brain with as many facts as you possibly can.
Your body has other ideas. It tells your mind that the **REAL** fact is, you should get some

quality kip in to recharge your batteries. And a good breakfast! So which side do you listen to? Do you say, 'Never, mind' or, 'No, body'?

The secret answer is … **NEITHER!** You should **listen to both**.

Like they say in the train announcements, you have to **mind the gap**. There's a way to close that gap, and that's known as making the **mind-body connection**. That sounds a bit *woo-woo*, but all it means is that you are always touching base with yourself – how you move and feel in your body and your head all the time. It's about not **ignoring** your mind **or** your body. Minding that gap really does help you become the **best you ever**.

My go-to thing is going barefoot in the grass. I might only have the one foot, but the feeling that washes over me (unless I step into something bad) is so, so good. Try it! You won't believe how good a little thing like that makes you feel.

REST STOP

Barefoot in the grass

See if my barefoot trick can work for you, too.
Take off your shoes and socks so you have bare
feet (if you can't do that, any bare body part will
do!) then go and stand outside for a few minutes
on a nice grassy patch. It can be wet or dry, warm
or cold – just close your eyes and focus on the
feeling of the grass on your bare skin. Maybe
it's spiky, maybe it's soft – either way you are
connecting with nature. See how you feel before
you do it, then again when you put your shoes
back on. It feels good, right?

This feeling is partly because it's nice to be in
nature, but also because of something amazing
called 'grounding'. Grounding, or 'earthing', is
when you connect your bare body (feet, hands,
elbows) with the ground. This lets the earth's
electrical currents flow into your body, which
can help reduce stress, pain or worry. Studies
have even shown that grounding can lower
inflammation and improve sleep!

Here's a little more about your bud, your bestie, your BFF ... aka, your brain. That wrinkly, cauliflower-shaped, 1.3 kilogram blob of wiggly jiggly stuff is so soft, it has to float inside liquid in your head so it doesn't bump into any bones. Your brain is **in charge** of all the things you don't think about that much, like breathing, but also things like thinking, moving and talking. What a hard worker!

YOUR BRAIN IS STUDENT OF THE MONTH, EVERY MONTH.

But how does this powerful organ control everything you think, do, feel and say? Remember a few pages back, when I said you were **atomic**? Well, you are also ELECTRIC. Shocking, I know!

Let me explain. Every physical experience or bodily function we have (seeing, smelling, hearing, moving, thinking, even your heart going *thud-thud-boom*) depends on **electrical impulses** in your body.
Yes, farting as well.

Important note: please don't attempt to plug yourself in. You are already charged up and ready.

You also remember how everything in our bodies is made of atoms, right? Ask your brain if you forgot. Anyway, to make atoms you need **special electrically charged particles** that are EVEN smaller than atoms! These are known as:

- **Protons** (positively charged, like me!)
- **Neutrons** (nice and neutral)
- **Electrons** (negative – *boo hiss* – but not AT ALL villains.)

OK, so far, so good. But HOW does it all work?

There's something called **action potential**. Sounds like a good movie, right? But it's actually when **positive ions** (i.e.. atoms with more protons in them than electrons, which gives them a positive charge) move in and out of special nerve cells called **neurons**. This activity sparks an electrical impulse – a signal or message – which is passed along from neuron to neuron (like a sort of brainy relay race) through connective bridges at the end of each neuron called **synapses**.

And it's these signals which fire away along neural pathways and through the synapses (which they do at an astonishing 120 metres per second), all around your brain, your body and back again, which help you to think, feel, move and talk. All of it done via **electricity**, and all without batteries! This is why the idea of 'grounding' is thought to make you feel so good – because it balances your body's electrical system, making you feel better.

Which is a relief since those are <u>not</u> included.

Would you believe that when the average person is lazing about on the sofa, their body still makes about 100 watts of power? That's the same as a **light bulb**.

FAST FACT:

It's thought that top athletes can produce up to 2,000 watts of power while sprinting. Imagine if you could run as fast as that. It's enough to see your name in lights!

Now let's talk about **synapses**! Woo! There are about a **quadrillion** in your brain. That's a million billion. Or a thousand trillion. It's a number so big, it hurts my head just thinking about it. What's going on there in your brain is way more complicated than even the internet. Every time you learn or do something, **EVEN READING THIS BOOK,** you make new connections between synapses, like adding a new line to the Tube network that is your brain. I wonder what the map would look like?

This brain stuff is way more complicated than that, and I'd love you to learn more about it, but that's enough for now. ←

Otherwise your brain might short-circuit!

BACK TO THE BODY.

Anyone who's ever had a smelly PE kit (and that would include me) knows that you can train to be **fitter**, **stronger** and **healthier**.

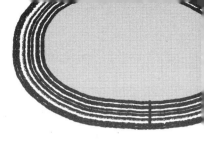

TRAINING IS A GINORMOUS PART OF MY LIFE.

I usually hit the track for a couple of hours a day, but sometimes I'm there for more like five hours, stretching, running, jumping and lifting weights. (Don't worry, I still make time for Xbox, too.)

Anyway, when you move your body, you don't just build muscles – **YOU MAKE THE SYNAPSES IN YOUR BRAIN STRONGER.** Your brain listens to the signals you send from your body. If you do something different, it builds new connections or re-jigs the ones that are already there. And the more you do it, the stronger those connections become. In a nutshell:

YOUR BRAIN CAN AFFECT YOUR BODY IN GOOD WAYS OR BAD WAYS, AND WHAT WE DO WITH OUR BODIES CAN AFFECT OUR BRAINS IN GOOD WAYS OR BAD WAYS.

That's the mind-body connection again. A **dynamic duo** for sure.

> **"Mental will is a muscle that needs exercise, just like muscles of the body."**
>
> – Lynn Jennings

On a typical training day, I have to set about three alarms, five minutes apart. I am not that much of a snoozer, it's more that waking up is not one of my **strong** points. But I make myself get up, have some eggs and hit the track. I admit, my head isn't always into it right away. Mental will? Sometimes it's more like mental *won't*. But **no brain, no gain**. The point is, the more I've done it, the easier it has become.

And you know what? No matter what, it never fails to make me feel **happy**.

Because that's another thing getting active helps with: feeling **happy**. I once had the chance to help out for an initiative called **Every Body Moves** where we tried to get more people with disabilities into sports by linking up those people with brilliant sporting opportunities. It was a really important initiative because it was all about how being active makes you feel **happier**. And what could be more important than helping people find their smiles?

What I'm saying is that getting a move on doesn't just keep your body fit, it keeps your brain healthy and in tip-top shape for doing its **thinking, learning** and all that **happiness stuff I've been going on about**. Want to know more?

Time to dive back into the science stuff.

Meet another top couple: **serotonin** and its buddy **dopamine**. *Pay attention. These two will be back!*

Serotonin is a neurotransmitter. (**A WHAT?** That's a special chemical in your brain, blood and digestive system that your neurons use to talk to each other.) Serotonin is like a smiley emoji. It says to your brain and body, 'Don't worry, keep going, be happy!'.

Dopamine is another neurotransmitter (a lot of those about!) that helps you feel full of energy and happy thoughts. You can imagine its emoji as a smiley face with sunglasses on, because too much of it is not ideal.

I also want you to meet the top dog, the main cheese, the big fish (or porpoise), the head honcho. Another neurotransmitter that makes you feel GREAT. **Endorphins**.

Endorphins are not at all related to dolphins or porpoises (as cool as that would be). They're actually more chemicals in your brain that make any pain or stress you have go away. You get them from doing **exercise**. If we're running with the porpoise joke, just think of it a bit like a dolphin or porpoise splashing about and releasing happy waves.

Your brain wants to make you feel **good**.
So if you feel upset, stressed out, miserable, or in pain, your brain notices. It tells you to do something good for yourself and rewards you for it. Exercise is always a winner when it comes to releasing endorphins, but did you know that just smiling or laughing can release them too? Now that's pretty **cool**. Thank you, brain.

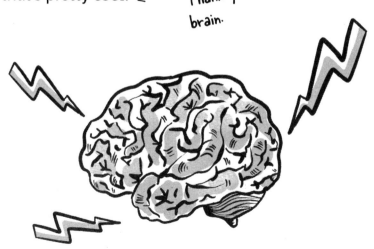

Happiness Hack

Mood booster

Try one physical activity in a short burst and see how you feel before and after doing it.

You could try:

- Running or moving around on the spot for 30 seconds (or a whole minute if you can hack it)

- Doing 10 or even 20 jumping jacks in a row — if you're using a wheelchair and it isn't equipped with hydraulics, try flapping your arms like a bird for one minute instead!

- Moving from one end of the room to the other in whatever way you can think of as quickly as you can

- Challenging a friend to some kind of race — I suggest a one-legged race!

Pay attention to your breath and pulse before and after too. Do you notice any differences?

THE THING ABOUT YOUR BODY IS THAT IT'S JUST LIKE A BIG, WALKING, TALKING BATTERY.

And batteries need **recharging**. So, as much as you need to boost your body with regular exercise, you also need to give it time to recharge. (Bad luck, this doesn't mean you can play on screens all evening!) Recharging means doing **mindful activities** such as walking or quietly thinking about things – which helps you rest your body and brain so you can get a good night's sleep.

"It's not about the number of hours you practise, it's about the number of hours your mind is present during the practice."
– Kobe Bryant

I hope I don't sound too much like a robot who never switches off when I say: train, relax brain, train, relax brain. You do need a **break** – not just sometimes, but all the time. Life isn't planned or perfect, in a robotic way. Sometimes it throws you a **curveball** that knocks you off your feet, and you have to pick yourself up, realise you're still here and carry on the best you can.

As well as breaks, it's also important to have things or people in your life who can bolster you and help you turn off the **sprinty stuff**. I am lucky enough to have my dogs who jump on me when I get home. And a great family and girlfriend. And video games.
And peri-peri chicken. ↗

Do you remember that stuff about mindfulness we talked about? I hope you were **mindful** of it. Anyway, it hopefully makes sense now that you know a bit more about how things *work*. You can do lots of physical stuff to help you calm down, focus and be happy. But another way to do this is through **grounding exercises**. They're brilliant for when you are feeling anxious, nervous or worried.

Laura (remember our wonderful happiness coach), has given us a few examples of these on page 234, but here's one to try now:

SIX STEPS TO UNWIND

Getting in tune with your body is easy. Follow these steps to dive deep within yourself.

1. Sit somewhere quiet. It could be on your favourite sofa, on a park bench or in your garden.

2. Take a slow, deep breath in through your nose for five seconds, hold for seven seconds and exhale for eight. Let the air WHOOOOOOOOOOSH out of your mouth.

3. Now, take in your surroundings. Think about what you can see. Pick out tiny details that you wouldn't normally notice.

4. Think about what you can hear. Focus on the sounds around you. How many can you count?

5. Next, think about what you can feel. What is touching your body? Where is there pressure? Can you feel your heartbeat?

6. As you breathe slowly in and out, think about all the things around you. Let your mind wander as you enjoy this calm moment to pause and connect with your surroundings and yourself.

See how you felt before doing this and how you felt after. Do you feel better than you did before?

Find more of these on page 234.

Now, I've talked a lot about easy and soothing activities to help with your mind-body connection.

BUT WHAT ABOUT TRYING SOMETHING COMPLETELY UNSOOTHING AND SHOCKING (AND, TO SOME, FRANKLY QUITE HORRID)?

Using **cold water** to boost your mood and your body has become very popular. Lots of people swear by it, talking about all sorts of benefits, like feeling happier and healthier, having less muscle soreness, worrying less and feeling more awake! Want to try it?

⟍ Are you sure?!

REST STOP

Freeze your bum off

OK, these activities are only for the bravest amongst you. So dig deep! It's about shocking your body into a different state, and freeing up your mind to find a new mind-body connection. So I'll give you a couple of different levels:

Level 1 – Ice bucket challenge!

You might need to get someone to help you with this one so you don't chicken out. Ready? Get a big bucket filled with ve-e-ery cold water and lots of ice, then sit down (probably outside) and pour the whole lot over your head! It's brutal and freezing but oddly brilliant for your mind and your body.

Level 2 – Cold water showers! (YOU WHAT!?)

Now this takes a little more bravery. In fact, try not to think too much about it or you'll probably back out. But next time you're in a funk (or even if you're not), get in the shower and try turning the temperature riiiiiiight down. Stand under that cold water as long as you can bear it (but no longer than two minutes or I'll get in trouble for turning you into a popsicle). Eventually your body will stop screaming at you to get out, and you might even enjoy it. BRRRR!

Iceman

Shout out to Dutch endurance athlete, Wim Hof. Or, as his fans know him, the Iceman.

He taught me to take a **FREEZING COLD** shower every day. The brrrrrrrrrr just gets you going and you feel so good! It's addictive. I even had to call the front desk in a hotel I was staying in to complain that the shower wasn't cold enough. Cold bum and body = alert brain and less pain. A frosty thanks to Wim.

Now, remember that exam that was bugging you, and the argument between your brain and your body? One solution would be to go outside for a walk. Simple, right? But go slow,

think about how every step feels and listen to all the stuff around you. Maybe birds singing, maybe sirens screaming, it doesn't really matter. Another solution might be to be brutal with yourself and get out the ice bucket or run on the spot for a minute or two! Either way, **being aware** will help you to calm your nerves.

JUST MIND THAT GAP.

> *"Only when our clever brain and our human heart work together in harmony can we achieve our full potential."*
>
> – Dr Jane Goodall

Grabbing greatness

Here's a task where we can see the mind-body connection in action. All you have to do is ... be grateful.

To do this, I want you to create a gratitude habit that you try and complete every day. This way, we're linking up our mind (because we're thinking of things we're grateful for) with our body (because gratitude sends those happy hormones I mentioned before around our brain).

To activate those happy hormones, I want you to think about three things you're grateful for today. If it helps, you can try to think of the below. Coach Laura calls this the 'three great things' approach:

- One thing about yourself you are grateful for
- One person you are grateful for
- And one experience you have been grateful for

Building habits that make our brain feel good can really help us to feel great. But how can you make a gratitude habit each day? Try this gratitude timetable and give Laura's 'three great things' approach a try!

One thing I'm grateful to me, my body or my brain for:

One person I'm grateful for:

One experience I'm grateful for:

RACE PLAN: *LAP FOUR*

What are you grateful for?

Write down three things you're grateful for. You can use the 'three great things' idea from the previous page or just choose three random ideas. Then think about when you plan to practise being grateful or your 'three great things' exercise. Try to do it every day. What time will you choose?

You can use this space for any notes you want to make about what you've learnt in this chapter!

CHAPTER FIVE

CHANGE YOUR LANE, CHANGE YOUR GAME!

CHANGE YOUR LANE CHANGE YOUR GAME!

This chapter is all about **zoning out**.

No, no, no. That is **not an invitation to go take a long, snoozy nap**, unless your brain and body are telling you that you need one. If that's the case, you might want to have a pillow fight with them and see who wins.

When I say 'zone out', I'm talking about **jumping right out of one zone and into another**! ← _Not the comfy one!_
In other words, try doing something new!

Remember when we did that Future You brain dump on page 81, thinking about **ALL** the things you might like to try and maybe even be good at? (I'm afraid to say napping shouldn't be included here.

It is **TOO EASY** to be good at that, especially with my cuddly dogs around.) Well, maybe now is the time to try your hand at one of them – maybe even one that you **MIGHT NOT** be good at.

With a bit of luck, that brain dump will have helped you understand a bit more about what you love and what you can do. SO in that case ... **whoosh**!

CHANGE IT UP!

Get that Moustachioed Magician back from chapter two to pull the tablecloth out from under your fish and chips. Just watch out for the ketchup.

REST STOP

Switch things around

Jumping out of your comfort zone can sound scary. After all, when you know what you're good at, you'd be mad to spend time on something you're not good at, right? **Wrong!**

Trying new things can be fun as well as scary, and sometimes you need to be a little bit brave. But if you do anything enough times, you'll get good at it.

Don't believe me? Try writing the line 'I can do new things' with the hand you don't normally use to write. Now write the same words with your usual hand. See the difference?

It's much easier with your usual hand because you have already made those brain connections – you practise them all the time. BUT the more you try writing with your other hand – the 'wrong' hand – the easier that will become too. It's all just about practice. And this is the same for everything that you try to do.

The funny word used to classify the kind of race I used to run in with my disability. I now run in the T64 class. Confusing — I know!

At the 2016 Summer Paralympics in Rio de Janeiro, Brazil, I won gold in the T44 100 metres in just **10.81 seconds**!

PROBABLY ABOUT THE SAME TIME IT JUST TOOK YOU TO READ THAT LAST SENTENCE.

That serotonin was firing! I was feeling pretty great. Thanks, serotonin!

People noticed me. In a good way. Then not long after, in the autumn of 2017, something totally unexpected happened. I was invited to join *Strictly Come Dancing*. You know, that TV show where people partner up (just like serotonin and dopamine, ha ha) to compete against each other in **ballroom dancing**. My comfort zone? I was so far out of it I couldn't even **SEE** it anymore.

My mates were **astounded**, to say the least. Because my dancing skills were ... let's just say, **not quite gold-medal winning**. If the show was called *Strictly Come <u>Dad</u> Dancing*, I probably would have had a good shot. So being asked to take part in something like this felt **way harder** than being asked to do a running race with only one leg! By now, sprinting was familiar to me so I was already good at it. That's why I do it.

BUT IT WAS TIME TO STEP OUT OF MY ZONE.

"You have to get out of your comfort zone in order to grow."
— **Octavia Spencer**

Happiness Hack

Try something new

Right, ready to do it yourself? Make yourself a plan to try something new. It could be anything — from talking to someone new at break time, to picking a different seat at the lunch table. You could try a new sport or hobby, or taste a new food or drink.

Maybe try and choose something that aims to achieve some of the goals that you set yourself in chapter three? It doesn't matter how small the new thing is — even one tiny change can grow a huge amount of confidence.

Try to make a note of how you felt before trying the new thing and how you felt after trying it. What do you notice?

Come on – we have talked about how

TRYING NEW THINGS IS GOOD FOR YOUR BODY AND YOUR BRAIN.

Yes, it's a little bit tough trying new things because you've got to **practise**. But remember,

YOU ARE UNIQUE! You have skills. Make the most of them, in new ways. Find new things. Throw yourself into it. Even though I was really good at sprinting when I was asked to be on *Strictly Come Dancing*, I didn't want to be stuck doing *just* that.

I WANTED TO GROW AND LEARN – AND SEE WHAT ELSE I WAS CAPABLE OF.

So when I said yes, I was never expecting to win. That was never the point. I just knew that if I mixed things up, my brain would **notice** – in a **positive** way. I'd make some more synapse connections, really shiny, glittery, dancey ones.

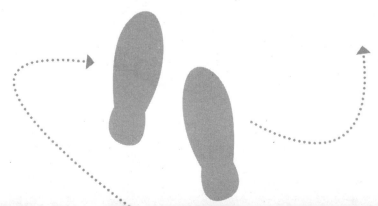

FAST FACT:

Every time you do something new, your brain creates a new neural pathway. (Remember all those neurons sending messages and signals along the pathways in your brain? Here they are in action!) Then the next time you do that same thing, it gets easier. That's why the first time we try something new it is hard, but after that it keeps getting easier and easier.

The other thing was, I wanted to silence anyone's ideas about me, and show them that the reason I was a bad, or Dad, dancer was not because I had a disability.

IT WAS BECAUSE I WAS A TERRIBLE DANCER.

You can't just look at someone and put them in a box.

Oti Mabuse

My dance partner on *Strictly Come Dancing* was not only the best dance partner a guy could ask for – supporting me while I stepped so far out of my comfort zone it felt like I'd moved to outer space. But she's also someone who stepped out of her own comfort zone to do the thing that truly makes her happy: dancing. Oti trained to be an engineer at university but soon after graduating, she decided it wasn't for her. So she made the bold choice to change lanes and move to Europe, where she became a competitive Latin and ballroom dancer. And she's been dancing ever since!

What an experience! I can honestly say that during my time on *Strictly Come Dancing* **my brain grew the most ever**. I learned **so much** through trying something new and completely different from anything I'd done before.

Saying **yes** to everything from the make-up and fake tan to the fancy shoes and sparkly outfits was such a laugh. I loved every moment of it – I just stopped taking myself too seriously and had **fun**. (Well, *wearing* the fake tan was fun. Waking up with orangey-brown-striped bedsheets was a bit of a shock to the system.)

It might have looked a little bit like something else ... if you know what I mean!

Anyway, it just goes to show, IT'S WORTH TRYING NEW THINGS.

Giving things a go can **build your self-confidence** and **open your outlook** to everything out there in life. Maybe it's a small switch, say, from football to sprinting. Maybe it's a giant challenge like learning a language or an instrument. Who knows? It might be brilliant fun. It might open doors.

Just look at me. Not only did I go from **sprinter** to **ballroom dancer**. I'm also Jonnie Peacock, **author**. As someone who wasn't a massive reader at school, I stepped out of my comfort zone and created this book. It's been a **challenge**, and something I knew nothing about when I started, but it's been an amazing, mind-bending experience and opened my brain up to so much. Yes, it's been scary. I have no idea if anyone is going to read this. ← *Apart from you!* But I did it, and that's what **matters**.

DON'T BE AFRAID THAT YOU MIGHT STUMBLE AND FALL.

Your brain is on your side (unless it lost the pillow fight) and will love your **boldness**. Serotonin and dopamine (there they are again!) will give you a mental high-five. And the more experiences you have, the more likely it is you'll discover **what really makes you happy**.

> *"Just try new things. Don't be afraid. Step out of your comfort zones and soar, all right?"*
>
> – Michelle Obama

One last thing to say is:

DON'T LET YOUR BRAIN TALK YOU OUT OF THINGS.

There's this thing called a **mindset**. It's the way you think and make opinions about all the stuff you encounter in the big, wide world. And there's a little hint in the name that tells you to **be wary of the scary**. It's that word: 'SET'. Set reminds you of standing still, not moving on, never changing, never being open to **un-setting**! Like setting the table and never tidying it up again. And if you're set in your ways, you can't grow. Make sure your mindset turns into a **growth mindset** –

ONE THAT LETS YOU DO ANYTHING!

Tidy up your table and grow your brain.

SO, STEP OUTSIDE YOUR ZONE. SPRINT OUTSIDE IT. AND RUN TOWARDS THE BEST YOU.

Bring a friend

When it comes to trying new things, bringing someone along for the ride can make a big difference. Think of a friend or family member who might want to try something new with you and ask them to join you — you'll be amazed how keen people are to try new stuff. You could inspire them! If you don't know yet what you want to try, you can come up with something together too. It takes two to tango.

Then once you have an idea, you can sit down and write out a plan for:

WHAT YOU'RE GOING TO DO
and
HOW YOU'RE GOING TO DO IT

Even planning things that you enjoy will release happy hormones in the brain (hello again, serotonin and dopamine!) so you will give yourself a happiness boost before you've even started!

If you want to really get out of your comfort zone, why not try making a new friend AND asking them to try something new with you? Two birds, one stone. Go on, you never know what could happen.

RACE PLAN: LAP FIVE
New things to try

Write down five new things you're going to try.
Then add a box to tick them off once you've
done them. Why not link these new things to the
goals you wrote down for chapter three? Do any
of them involve you trying something new?

You could even set yourself a plan for when
you're going to add new things to your list.
It could be the first of each month or the
twelfth (if that's your lucky number). Keep
adding to your list so your mindset keeps
growing and growing. Good luck!

You can use this space for any notes you want to make about what you've learnt in this chapter!

CHAPTER SIX

YOUR PERSONAL BEST!

I hope you are enjoying this sprint so far, and that you're thinking and learning a lot. Now I want to talk to you a bit about **PBs**. No, that doesn't stand for **peanut butter**. A PB, or personal best, in my world normally means an athlete's fastest time, highest score or best **ever** result. Just like the time I smashed the world record at London's 2012 Paralympics – **then broke my own record** in the Rio Paralympics four years later! Sorry, I'll stop showing off now because this is about **your** personal best. Not mine.

I know what you're thinking, *Brilliant, Jonnie's going to help me win all the prizes at sports day and help me beat my brother at running down the street*. But I'm actually not talking about *that* kind of personal best. Because guess what? We can't always be **better**, **stronger**, **faster** – but we can always **try** our best. And that's what this chapter is all about.

Now, I don't want to be Joyless Jonnie here, but of course **things don't always go your way** – in races or in life. Sometimes it can seem like there are more 'I cannots' than 'I cans', and that stinks more than your socks.

—And mine!

> *"Don't be afraid of failure. This is the way to succeed."*
> – LeBron James

When you were little, did you ever worry about monsters under the bed? I know I did. When you get older, the monsters have names: **anxiety**, **fear**, **worry**. And there is probably the odd smelly sock down there, making everything more monstrous. But those monsters are here for a reason:

TO MAKE YOU STRONGER.

"You have to remember that the hard days are what make you stronger. The bad days make you realise what a good day is. If you never had any bad days, you would never have that sense of accomplishment!"

– Aly Raisman

REST STOP

Try and try again

Think of a time when you tried something and didn't get the result you wanted. Focus for a minute on <u>why</u> that happened. Maybe something went wrong, maybe your mind was elsewhere, maybe you hadn't practised enough or maybe it just wasn't your day? Whatever the reason, it's easy to let the experience fill you with anxiety, fear and worry. And these can eat away at you and take away your confidence. BUT, don't let them hold you back! Use the experience to help you to learn. Often by having an awareness of why something didn't go to plan means that next time you know which area to improve on. Try doing it again. And then again. **Eventually, you'll nail it!**

I still have monsters. And I fight them all the time.

Now, I don't want to make this book a 'heartwarming story about overcoming bad things', but, tell you what? Losing my leg actually helped me find my **ambition**. Yes, it was super tough for my family. When I was rushed to hospital back in 1998, some doctor-type people thought I was going to die.

I know, I'm old!

They put me in a coma for a week and told everyone to prepare for the worst. **Thankfully** I pulled through – removing my leg was the only way of saving my life. Once I'd realised what had happened, it felt **extremely bad**, but people made me realise I was one of the lucky ones. And my mum taught me that you can't let anything stop you, or your **dreams**. And even if she sometimes said she wished I would 'stop it!' (stop moaning, stop being lazy, stop avoiding chores), she *never* meant **stop** dreaming.

It took me a while to figure all this out when I was a little kid, but I learned to **be brave**, to **work hard** and to **push** – even if my leg was **red raw from chafing** after running around all over the place.

MUM USED TO SAY THAT THE PAIN OF NOT BEING INVOLVED WOULD BE WORSE THAN THE PAIN OF A SORE LEG.

How right!

FAST FACT:

When babies are learning to walk, they don't give up when they keep falling over. They just keep trying again and again, until – at last – they can walk! Some research suggests that babies fall over 17 times an hour when learning. Good thing they have big soft nappies to protect their bums!

Here's a little story for you. Pull up a chair! I held onto my gold for the 100 metres at the Rio Paralympics in 2016. But then that golden cookie started to crumble. I'd start off strong on track during practice, but after I got to about 50 or 60 metres, I began to get an **intense pain**.

Shortbread? Yum!

Turns out my blade wasn't actually fitting properly and was the reason I was struggling to compete. It was causing me so many problems and so much pain.

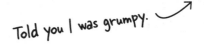

IT GOT SO BAD THAT I STOPPED LOVING WHAT I DO BEST.

I felt grumpy, cross and off balance, in my body, my leg AND my head. I kept thinking, *WHY do I not have a foot down there like I should do? Why isn't this easier, when I have worked so hard? All the hours, days, weeks of training come down to seconds – and now this?*

Told you I was grumpy.

I was so excited for the Tokyo 2020 Paralympics (that actually took place in 2021). I was seeing **gold**.

But honestly, they were not my **best** games. My blade still wasn't working properly. And, of course, there was the complication of lockdown during the Covid-19 pandemic. That was a nightmare for everyone, but it really did take my **spark** away. I felt like I was just following instructions and going through the **motions**.

The Great British team were in **isolation** all together in the **Tokyo Olympic Village**. (Other countries had different rules for their teams, with more freedom to move about.) It was great being with my teammates, but really strange, too. British athletics booked us into a hotel right across from an **amusement park** to help us unwind but we weren't allowed to leave the hotel. So, we could only watch through the windows as everyone else had **fun**. *Seriously rubbish.*

Then, to make matters worse, at a race in 2023 I found out I had something called hamstring tendinopathy. Now, that is a fancy name for a **pain in the bum** – it's right at the top of your hamstring muscle in your thigh where it attaches to the pelvis bone you sit down with. And it was a pain in the bum in all kinds of ways.

LIFE! WHAT A ROLLER COASTER, RIGHT?

> *"I've missed more than 9,000 shots in my career. I've lost almost 300 games. Twenty-six times I've been trusted to take the game-winning shot and missed. I've failed over and over and over again in my life. And that is why I succeed."*
>
> – Michael Jordan

So I had some work to do. Deep down in my bum ...
I mean, mind ... I knew the combo of injury and blade
malfunctions was making me **unhappy**, and this was
keeping me away from my dream of chasing the **best
version of me**. I felt so down on myself.

SO I TURNED TO THE ONE THING THAT ALWAYS PUTS ME IN A BETTER MINDSET: EXERCISE.

Not the sprinting-to-win, pushing-myself-to-pain kind
of exercise I'd grown accustomed to. But the kind of
exercise where I wasn't pushing for a specific time or
outcome. The kind where I let my brain **breathe** and
my body just move. Every time I did something active,
even for just 15 minutes, I felt better.

Happiness Hack

Shake it out!

I picked up this tip online and I use it when my brain feels heavy and full of fog. I stand up and shake away the fog. Using my hands and whole body to banish it. You can jump around, wave your arms, shake your head. Whatever you do – get your body moving. Then go back to your day. See how you feel before and after trying this out. Fog free, I hope.

If you understand what **motivates** you, you really can do anything. Yep, I lost my mojo for a while, but the **fire** came back. Not literally! We are all safe.

I just said to myself, I love this life. I love what I do. But I have to **work** to make good things happen. My sport is moving on, my rivals are stepping up and getting better, and I should **evolve**, too.

After many more months of training, I started to turn things around. I was getting back to the times I used to hit. My brain was getting **fitter**, too. With the **support** of everyone around me, I started to turn my frown upside down.

It's far easier to sit on the couch and watch endless Netflix or play 10 hours of video games, and that is what I really wanted to do. But if I had, I'd have felt even more **moany** and **mopey**. Just getting a move on and doing something active stopped me from feeling worthless. I knew that by eating well, sleeping well and shaking it all about, I would feel so smiley and happy for the rest of the day.

FAST FACT:

It takes approximately 13 muscles to smile. You actually use more muscles frowning! So when you're tired from doing all that exercise, knowing this should give you another good reason to wear a cheery grin!

Pulling yourself out of a slump by exercising isn't just something that works for me.

IT'S SCIENTIFICALLY PROVEN TO WORK FOR EVERYONE!

Remember those **endorphins** I told you about in chapter four? Well, they come out to play when you get your heart rate up. Alongside that dancing duo, **serotonin** and **dopamine**. Remember them?

⤸ I hope so! I've gone on about them enough.

So if you're feeling like something hasn't gone your way, or just feeling down in the **dumps**, try and do something to **change your mind**. It doesn't have to be hard – you could just run up and down the stairs ten times. Or go outside and flap your arms about in the fresh air. You could go for a walk or bike ride. Or if you really feel like challenging yourself, you could go for a little run or swim. Anything like that will **fire up your energy** – and it will fire up your mood too.

AND THAT WILL GIVE YOU THE STRENGTH TO GO BACK AND TRY AGAIN AT WHATEVER IT WAS THAT MADE YOU GLUM IN THE FIRST PLACE.

Motivational magic

One of the hardest things about being in a slump is that it is very hard to motivate yourself. Sometimes you can't imagine anything worse than getting up and being active. SO — try writing Future You a mini motivational letter that is your go-to whenever you need to get yourself going.

The letter can be super short, saying something like:

Dear me,

I know you don't want to go for a walk, but I promise you will feel amazing afterwards!

Love from me

X

Or

Dear me,

I bet this TV show is really thrilling, but why don't you watch the rest later and go play football in the park instead? Last time we played, I had so much fun and slept so well after. The TV show can wait!

Love from me

X

You could even try writing different letters depending on what kind of exercise you'd like to try. I'd suggest writing your first few letters after you've done something active that has made you feel good. Think of all the feelings you have afterwards then write them down.

I like to tell myself that I never regret it if I do some exercise. You might not feel like it in the moment, but you'll definitely feel better afterwards. Sometimes Present You just needs a little nudge.

You know how we've been talking about that mind-body connection? Let's circle back to that again. Think of your brain as your slimy yet **super-secret weapon**. You can even give it a cool spy name if you want. Your brain's top-secret mission:

TO PROTECT YOU FROM SETBACKS AND GIVING UP, AND TO HELP YOU REMEMBER ALL THOSE SKILLS AND CONNECTIONS YOU'VE LOADED INTO YOUR MIND BANK.

Shhhhhhh! Spy brain!

Lots of people have studied how our brains secretly work to help us be good at things. They've identified something called a **fixed mindset** (remember meeting mindsets on page 142?) and it can really be a pain in the bum, even if it's in your head (if you know what I mean). The fixed mindset can make us feel **negative**. *I can't do this, I'm bad at that, I'll never get the hang of this thing, I'll mess this up for sure and everyone will have a laugh, I don't know what I'm talking about*. Those sorts of feelings.

BUT HERE IS THE SECRET BEHIND YOUR SECRET WEAPON: A GROWTH MINDSET.

That sounds like something injected into your brain in a science-fiction movie, but it's not. A growth mindset **turns that frown upside down**, in simple words. All those negative thoughts become positive ones.

I can do this if I practise. I don't know I'm bad at something until I give it a good go. I can get the hang of this once I've put in the effort, so bring it on. I might make a mistake, oops I did it again, but I might just nail it next time. I DO know what I am talking about, because it's me. Go on, challenge me.

YOU CAN'T WIN THE RACE UNLESS YOU ARE IN IT.

Super Sally

I'm sorry to make this a bit gushy, but this felt like the perfect moment to shout out my girlfriend, Sally Brown. If there is anyone who's been through challenges and carried on despite them all, it's her. A fellow Paralympic sprinter, she has always given the competition her all even when injuries and illness (including appendicitis, ouch!) got in her way. In the end, she didn't make it to Rio or Tokyo, but that hasn't stopped her. She still competes and is also now a model, working to give better visibility to people with disabilities. Her personal best is to keep doing what she loves, no matter the outcome. What could be cooler than that?

You can't take a magic potion to change your mindset.

YOU HAVE TO PUT THE EFFORT IN AND ACCEPT THAT NEGATIVE THOUGHTS, MESS-UPS AND FAILS CAN TURN INTO POSITIVE RESULTS.

As I write this, I am getting ready for the **Paris 2024 Paralympics,** and let me tell you for sure, the **brain training** is just as critical as the **body training**. I've put my head down and I'm focusing on my **goal** over anything else. Doing whatever I need to do. Including eating gummy sweets (which I can ACTUALLY EAT as part of my training routine).

I know! Good, right?

It helps too that Paris just happens to be my **favourite place** outside the UK.

As our happiness coach Laura says, **YOUR THOUGHTS BECOME YOUR FEELINGS AND SHAPE YOUR ACTIONS.** So the below is a little thought for YOU, based on **turning the negative into the positive.**

FAIL: **F**irst **A**ttempt **I**n **L**earning

END: **E**ffort **N**ever **D**ies

NOPE: **N**ext **O**pportunity, **P**lease, **E**lvis

(or something else that starts with an **E**!)

Keeping my brain and my body fit might lead me to gold. But getting ready for Paris 2024 is not all *ooh-la-la*. I have been **training** for so many hours I've lost count. Everyone I work with, from nutritionists to physiotherapists to coaches to my dogs, are doing **everything** they can to get me to the starting line. I know I have everything I need to succeed, and I hope I will. It'll be frustrating if I don't get there but I know I've done what I can. Who knows, by the time you read this I might have won my third gold medal. Or I might not have. And you know what? **Either way, I'll be OK.**

This is all to say that with the right mindset, YOU can reach your personal best. And no, that doesn't mean being the fastest, strongest, record-winner. It's about trying your best, and being happy with yourself that you've done something for you. Keep **trying**, keep **going**, keep **smiling** and REMEMBER THAT SECRET WEAPON IN YOUR HEAD.

FAST FACT:
Scientists have found what they believe to be the best temperature for happiness. A recent study found that the perfect temperature for humans is 22°C. It's thought that when we're at this temperature, we're more likely to have a positive mindset and feel happier.

A mantra for personal bests

Sometimes, our brains can be our own worst enemies. But what did I say about that growth mindset? One way to tell our brains to quieten down is to come up with our own positive affirmations or mantras (remember those sprints from page 93?). You can say these to yourself when things go wrong (and, sorry to break it to you, they will!), so you can pick yourself up again and keep on trying. They can be personal to you or quotes you've heard from someone you admire.

You could make them rhyme or turn them into a song. You could even write something that starts with each letter from FAIL or SUCCESS. It's your mantra, so do whatever you want with it.

Here are just a few ideas:

- I will keep trying and learning

  Starting simple.

- I can only do my best, if I have done my best the setbacks are a lesson, not a failure

- I am only competing with myself; this is a personal journey. My successes cannot be overshadowed or outdone by anyone else but me

- I won't give up if I'm stuck in a rut! *Ignore my terrible rhyming skills, but you get the idea!*

- I know that thing didn't go the way I wanted it to, but a FAIL is just a First Attempt in Learning. I'll try again and see what happens

- Making mistakes leads to lessons which lead to success, every setback is a positive step even when they feel like a failure

  Oh God, how did my editor let me keep this one!

- Failing Animals Inspire Laughter

When you can feel yourself getting in a funk, repeat your mantras and <u>believe</u> them! Whatever your affirmation – say it, learn it and keep repeating it. Remember: You can do anything!

RACE PLAN: *LAP SIX*

My affirmations

Write down three affirmations or mantras you will use when something doesn't go your way. Will you write your own or use one from the previous page? How will you use them to make you feel better?

You could make a poster of one of them. Look at the chapter openers designed by our incredible illustrator Ashwin to inspire you to make something fun, memorable and eye-catching that you can use over and over again.

You can use this space for any notes you want to
make about what you've learnt in this chapter!

CHAPTER SEVEN

The TEAM BEHIND YOUR DREAM!

THE TEAM BEHIND YOUR DREAM!

When you sprint, you run tall. You keep your **elbows bent** and **move your arms front to back**. No time for an armpit check, but hopefully you are not too smelly. And what does that matter anyway? Make sure your **knees stay high**. Put your feet right beneath you and don't step too far ahead. **Get those smelly socks moving**!

ALL THOSE THINGS, YOU HAVE TO DO BY YOURSELF.

And yep, I compete in what is called an individual sport. If you smelled some of my kit after a race, you would understand why it is good to be individual straight away. Phew! But the real truth is that I didn't (and you won't) get the furthest I could by working alone. **It's the team around you that gets you there.**

> ***"Individually,***
> ***we are one drop.***
> ***Together, we are***
> ***an ocean."***
>
> **– Ryunosuke Satoro**

Good memory!

You might be thinking, *Oi, this book is supposed to be about me. You definitely told me that all the way back on page 15!* And you are right. **But everyone needs support**. You are one person, unless you are a multi-headed hydra from mythology – an unlikely-reader type of monster. Although, if you had a couple of heads you could read two books at once. Both of them mine, I hope.

ANYWAY, I could never have ever got to where I am today without a team. **Not even close to the starting line**.

TEAMWORK JUST WORKS. WHY?

A

It is just so much easier to reach a goal when you **work together** with people you like and trust. You don't have to always agree with them, but that is part of the whole teamwork thing. Understand that they might have a **different** way of getting from A to B, one that might even involve G or some other letter. I picked that a bit randomly. But I hope you see what I mean.

Listen to what they have to say. Accept that they are **unique**, just like you are. (See how we keep going back to the starting line in this book?) Consider how great it is to have other people **share in your goal**, and put in the work to get there, especially if you hit a wall. Not literally. Unless your goal is building a big wall.

B

It's a bit like this book. This book isn't just mine. Yes, it's full of my ideas, my story. It was my concept. But I've **worked with a team to get it into your hands**. My literary agent, Lydia, who found me my publisher. My editor and designer, Emily and Katie, who've worked to transform it from idea into reality. Laura Earnshaw who brought her happiness expertise and Laura Buller who helped shape my words. Ashwin, who drew all the incredible illustrations. And **you**, my reader. Where would my book be without someone to read it? And (hopefully) laugh at all my stupid jokes.

REST STOP

Team you!

Who is on <u>your</u> team? Who makes you feel good and spurs you on when you need it? Who do you enjoy talking to you and gives you good advice? They might be relatives, teachers or friends – or they might be the nice lady at the post office down the road or your elderly neighbour. Write down their names, and then really think about what they do for you to make you feel happy. Sometimes by focusing on people, it helps you fully appreciate the support you have. Don't overlook them – **these people are your team.** Every single one of them.

Why not take it further and tell that person what they mean to you? And how you're glad to have them in your life. It will make their day and make you feel amazing. Being grateful (remember the Happiness Hack on page 124?) and spreading kindness releases your favourite double duo: dopamine and serotonin (not those two again!). Some people call this a 'helper's high'. Isn't your brain cool?

For me, a team means a few different things.

OF COURSE, MY FAMILY HAVE BEEN, AND STILL ARE, MY FIRST AND BEST TEAM.

I can't even begin to imagine the thoughts they must have had and the things they went through when I was ill. I'm in bits just imagining anything happening to my dogs! When the doctors put me in a coma and said, 'It's up to him now' – **that's when you rely on a team**. The **NHS team** to fix you, support you (and your scared family) and help you understand stuff so you can pull through, and your **family team** to keep a smile on your face.

SO THEY WERE MY FIRST TWO BIG TEAMS THAT MADE A BIG IMPACT ON MY LIFE.

Growing up I still had a bucket-load of **medical procedures** because my bones kept on growing, even though the rest of me was missing. I wasn't the best patient in the world. Every time I had a big procedure the doctors would have to put me to sleep beforehand. **I was scared**. I must have remembered that the last time I went under, I came back missing a part of myself.

Team Family

A huge shout out to my mum, Linda. Mum is a fighter, and she gave that spirit to me. I would need an **entire book** to thank her for always being on my team. Also on my family dream team are my dogs, Bella and Luna. Their wagging tails make any day a good day. And of course, my super sisters, Becka, Hanna and Beth. Becka likes to tell everyone that before my leg was amputated, she asked to have a little goodbye look. And, yes, she and Hanna had painted the toenails of that leg with golden glitter! They've always been my biggest supporters – on and off the race track.

My mum, Linda

When I got older, my **mates** became another big team for me. You know how we talked before about everyone wanting to be the same, even if they weren't? That is SO how I felt. I didn't want to get any brownie bonus points because I was missing a leg – I wanted to run and play and muck about with **everyone else**. I just wanted to get **involved**. And to everyone who helped me do that? Teamwork Gold.

And now, phew! From there, my team just gets bigger and bigger! I've had different **coaches** over the years (because sometimes teams grow and change), who have all been amazing and believed in me. I still work with my long-term coach, but now also have someone to help me with the **day-to-day training** as we build towards **Paris 2024**. I even have people who give me treatment before AND after I train. Dietitians, sports massage therapists, physiotherapists – you name it. (Then there's my Xbox, which is a key team player when it comes to helping me chill out after a tough morning on the track!)

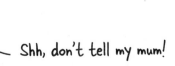

Shh, don't tell my mum!

I can't run faster until there is someone next to me, so my teammates on the track help me to go, go, GO! The entire Paralympic team **support each other** and **cheer each other** on. And you know what? Opponents are part of teamwork in a way, too – we respect each other and believe in each other, even if we want to WIN. You can see us hugging after a race. It's not fake, it is respect.

PLUS, YOU CAN'T WIN A RACE IF YOU'VE GOT NO ONE TO RACE WITH.

Then I have the marvellous magical team who created my running blade. It's built out of a super clever material called **carbon fibre** which is designed to be strong **AND** flexible at the same time. So when my foot hits the ground, my blade bends like a spring and then shoots me forward – basically copying what the muscles in my other leg do.

In case this sounds like cheating, heads up – it's not nearly as efficient as my other leg's muscles, but it's still pretty amazing!

Running blades are ve-e-e-e-ry complicated to make – they have to work right **AND** they have to fit the runner perfectly. To make my first blade, I had a team of more than **forty brilliant engineering people** working on it (yes, forty!), and it still took them **two years** to design and make it. Without their work, I could never have become a Paralympic gold medallist.

TEAMWORK REALLY IS DREAMWORK!

FAST FACT:

Ever wondered how the blade attaches to my stump without being bolted on? ← *Ouch!!*

Well, at the top of my blade is the socket, which is sort of like a sleeve that my stump goes into. Once I push my stump into the sleeve, all the air whooshes out of a valve and seals the sleeve around my knee. And once it's on, that blade isn't going anywhere! Cool, right? That's the brilliant engineering team for you.

Now, you might be thinking, *Hang on! I don't have a team! I'm not even IN a team! I hate football! (And running.)* But you do already have teams around you, like friends and family. As for joining an official team – like a local sports team, chess club or music group – that can sound like the SCARIEST thing ever. Perhaps you'd much rather go and shove your head down the toilet than even consider something like that.

BUT JUST WAIT!

Remember when I said **teamwork is dreamwork**? That's because joining a team is about so much more than learning a new skill. It's about meeting and connecting with people, and – even more importantly – GROWING YOUR OWN CONFIDENCE. There's **nothing like working together** to achieve something to fill you with a warm fuzzy glow and give you an instant confidence boost. Try it. You might surprise yourself.

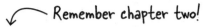
Remember chapter two!

So find the thing you love and see if there is a team out there for it. And it doesn't have to be a sports team! I know I've spoken **lots** about sports, because that's what **I** love, but there are so many other clubs you can join if you aren't keen on doing something active. How about an **adventurer's club** where you learn to camp in the woods? Or a **drama class** where you can train to become the next great Thespian?

And if you can't find a team you can join? You can **make one yourself**! It could be as simple as asking a group of people to create a football team or board game club and meet once a week. If you find you don't want to work with other people, try and figure out **why**. Then talk to your brain about those feelings and see if there is a way to push yourself despite that (getting out of the **zone**, remember chapter five?).

I KNOW IT CAN BE SCARY, BUT TRUST ME — IT'LL BE WORTH IT.

Power stance!

OK, so you've decided to bite the bullet and join a team. It's time to go and your mum is calling you, but your tummy has turned to jelly and your knees are knocking. This team-joining business is actually quite nerve-wracking. There's no way you can go feeling like this! It's time for a ...

POWER STANCE!

Now this may sound silly, but holding yourself in a ridiculously over-the-top position – you know, legs wide, hands on hips or doing strong arms, that kind of thing – can be a super confidence booster. Think of Superman! Or, have you ever seen the All Blacks rugby team perform The Haka? That is the ultimate moving power stance – it's like a dance but with fearsome power moves and loud noises. Try it! (You don't have to do the dance.)

Find a power stance that works for you, or make up your own, then do it when you feel nervous — you could even make a fierce roar if you like. Now — what are you going to do — stay home, or give it a go?

A WORD OF ADVICE:

If you have a disability and feel nervous joining a club for able–bodied people, don't panic. Nine out of ten times that's the advice I'd give anyone asking me how to get involved in parasport (or any club really!). Join an able–bodied club and watch your potential soar! Don't be afraid that you don't belong, because you do. And if you aren't sure the club or team will be able to work with you and your disability, just set up a meeting with the person running it or call ahead to talk it through. Normally, they will be keen to help you out and if they can't, they should be able to help you find somewhere else to join – be it a parasports team or another kind of supported club or group. I know this takes a little guts, but it's always worth it to try. Remember, just try to do what you WANT to do, always – you never know how it could change your life!

So what I hope this shows you is that **no one gets where they want without a team behind them**. Imagine me on a starting line-up for a race, with all the other athletes at the front on the starting blocks. In reality, there would be at least **ten people** behind every one of those sprinters! That would make for a very messy race! You'd have trainers, physios, doctors, managers, the people who make your running blades and more all trailing after you. Imagine it! You'd have people still tying their shoes, some faking injuries, many on the phone, coaches probably pulling their hair out, others having NO IDEA what to do. I am just being a bit silly here – it's

MY JOB to do the sprinting, and everyone else does an excellent job at what they do, but everyone sprinting? Maybe not.

You might not have a dozen-strong team helping you to get from A to B right now. You might *Most people won't!* never have a team as big as mine. ←

But **PEOPLE HELP CREATE WHO YOU ARE.**
That's why you need to surround yourself with people who believe in you . You don't want anyone to limit your potential. And other people see what you can't see in yourself. Like if your underpants are hanging out.

Keep good people, pets and friends around you. People who believe in you and support you.

AND YOU'LL GO FAR, I PROMISE.

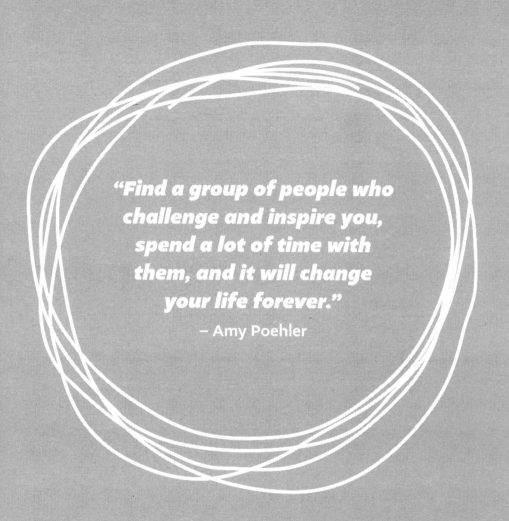

"Find a group of people who challenge and inspire you, spend a lot of time with them, and it will change your life forever."

– Amy Poehler

REST STOP

Build your dream team

This can be tricky. There are lots of people around. Who are the right ones to pick? Well, part of having a dream team is having a goal – you need to know what you are aiming for to know what you need from your team. So, let's break it down.

Step 1 – What do you want to achieve? It might be getting into a new sport, or taking your current skills to the next level, or even venturing into a team for the first time. But have a goal in mind.

Step 2 – Next, think about how you'll get there. What do you need to help you achieve your goal? Maybe you need someone to drive you to practice, or to force you to go when it's cold and rainy. Or just support you when you're not feeling it.

Step 3 – What characteristics do your teammates need to get the best out of you?

You don't want people on your team who aren't kind to you, or say mean things to you. You also probably don't want someone who would laugh if you made a mistake. Pick people who lift you up and make you feel great.

Step 4 – Now, time to assemble the dream team! Write down the names of the people who match the requirements above.
This is your team! These are the people who will pep you up, play alongside you and inspire you.

THESE ARE THE PEOPLE WHO WILL HELP YOU ACHIEVE YOUR GOAL.

Here's one extra bit of advice: always try to be a good teammate back. It takes a whole team working together, being kind to each other and supporting each other to make a **dream** team.

RACE PLAN: LAP SEVEN

Your team

Write down three people who are already on your team — who you know have your back and will support you no matter what. Then I want you to think about adding one new person to your team. They could be a new friend, someone you met at a club or someone famous you admire (and wish was on your team). Keep trying to add to and grow your incredible team, while being a good teammate to others. Remember, teamwork really is dreamwork.

You can use this space for any notes you want to make about what you've learnt in this chapter!

CHAPTER EIGHT

Pass it on!

PASS IT ON!

As we've sprinted (NOT TOO FAST!) through this book, I hope you've learned that when it comes to pursuing your dreams, there are ways to find what you **love**, whatever it is that you want to do and whatever your **circumstances**. Hopefully you've also learned that when you find those dreams, goals and loves, you need to **grab** them! Even if there is a koala trying to steal them or a porpoise ready to swim away with them. They're **yours**! Don't let naughty koalas or porpoises have them!

Finding what you love and growing it is one of the most important things you can learn to do in life. Not only does it make you feel **great**, but you can apply the tools you used to find those loves to almost anything. So you can keep growing, learning and **smiling**.

I know it sounds cheesy, but I feel **privileged** to think that I was (hopefully) able to help you get there. So, on that note, there's just one last thing I want to show you ...

You didn't think you were finished yet, did you?

There is something **even more** important than learning how to find what you love. And that is

HELPING SOMEONE ELSE TO FIND WHAT THEY LOVE. Because when you share, you'll not

only recap all the stuff you've learned – you'll also **give the gift of knowledge** to someone else.

> *"If you have knowledge, let others light their candles in it."*
> – Margaret Fuller

Can I tell you something? Not about moustaches, magicians, porpoises and rabbits. Possibly koalas though (just hide your valuables). It's about **sprinting**.

So, as you know, my main event is 100 metres, and my **fastest time so far is 10.64** seconds. In that time, you could tie your shoes. Or watch a traffic light cycle between green to yellow to red. Or tell your pet you love them and give them a nice scratch behind the ears. Or eat a couple of gummy sweets.

Result! ⟶

Given how quick that is, you'd think it would all go by in a blur. But when I'm racing, my thoughts are whizzing around metre by metre. I know exactly how I am doing – whether I'm where I should be, who is sneaking ahead of me and how I am going to execute and win. That's training for you!

Not in a scary murdering way, I already told you that!

But it wouldn't mean a thing if I didn't **pass my skills on to others** – including **you** with this book. In the previous chapter, we talked about the importance of teamwork. One of the most teamwork-y things you can do is **help and support people**, EVEN IF THEY ARE COMPETING AGAINST YOU.

Right, now it's your turn.

'What?! Wait just a minute!' I hear you say. You think because I am a gold-medal winner it is super easy for me to tell you that *Still sounds cool.* you should go and help someone. You're probably thinking, *But I've only just finished trying to find what I love without worrying about what someone else loves.* And yes, it is kind of tricky working on yourself, keeping going, learning and moving forwards – **AND THEN BEING TOLD TO START SHARING.**

But, remember – **I believe in you**. (And no one is asking you to go on TV to talk about it.) *Yet!* Let's start somewhere smaller. Think about **allyship** – about being a good friend and a good teammate. Passing on what you've learned can be as simple as **being there for someone** who's having a rough time. Have you seen how at the end of a race, we all hug, even though just seconds before we were bitter rivals on the track and **only one of us was the winner**? It's because we all want to say, 'Good job. You did the best you could, and you did great.'

FLOWERS CAN BLOOM AT DIFFERENT TIMES, BUT THEY ARE STILL FLOWERS.

Although I smell nothing like a flower after a race!

REST STOP

Open your eyes!

It's easy to get wrapped up in our own little worlds and not notice when people around us are struggling. Or sometimes it's easier not to look at all. Open your eyes – notice what is going on and support people when they need it.

Stick up for someone who's having a hard time or give someone a boost if they miss a goal, make a mistake, get picked on or lose a race.

If you notice someone going through something where you think they could do with support, why not try one of the below?:
- Ask if they are OK or if they want to talk
- Listen to them and see if there is anything you can do to help
- Bring them a gift or make them a card
- Speak to a grown-up if you think they can help

Sticking up for people is a great way of giving back!

Helping people **makes me feel good**. That's partly why I do it. But mostly I do it because I'm so lucky to have found what makes me happy and I want to share that feeling. For me, my running brings me joy, but for someone else it could be drawing or fixing things. And I want young people with disabilities to be able to find these things too, so they can enjoy sports or get involved in what they feel passionate about. TO FIND WHAT THEY LOVE THE MOST.

A few years ago, I made a programme called *Jonnie's Blade Camp*.

— ARRRGH!

Wait! No, not that kind of scary blade! The brilliant, clever, custom-made, carbon-fibre (remember that?) kind of blade, like the one I'm wearing on the cover of this book. Phew!

So this programme had five young people – the eldest was fifteen, the youngest only eight – and they had all lost either one or both of their legs. My job was to get them to realise that there was still a route to their goal – it just might take some creative thinking and a lot of will. But mainly my job was helping them to **believe in themselves**. And by the end, all five of those kids were able to achieve their sporting goals.

AND I HOPE FOR THEM IT WAS LIFE-CHANGING!

Not just because of their physical accomplishments, but because of the **self-confidence** and **self-belief** that they all gained. They all found what they were passionate about. And nothing could take that away from them.

Not even one of those naughty koalas.

And it was incredible for me to watch their progress and learn from them too. Because I **knew** how those kids felt. I was them. When I was seven, David Beckham completely inspired me and instilled in me my love of sport. And with *Jonnie's Blade Camp*, I felt so lucky to have had the chance to **pay that same kindness forward** to another **generation** of kids. Just like David did for me!

By pushing yourself forward, you make the **small steps**. Which is great! But I think you can only make the **giant leaps** when you give someone else a helping hand (or leg, or blade). TO HELP EVERYONE ELSE SO YOU CAN HELP YOURSELF.

Some people might try to pull you down, but others will **make things better**. Try and be one of the ones who make it better. Be kind and accepting of people with differences – whether it's a disability or a different skin colour or accent. Remember,

WE ARE ALL UNIQUE.

Happiness Hack

Acts of kindness

Another way to give back to those around you is by doing something kind for someone else. Want to give it a go?

Look at the people who support you. What can you do specifically to give them a boost? Remember, adults need a kind word every now and again, too. Giving them a hug or a hand with something (even something as mundane as hanging out the washing or cleaning their car) will make their day!

Maybe pick a week and call it 'Kindness Week' – then aim to do one nice thing each day during that week. Walk the neighbour's dog, let your little sister practise her goalie skills with you or hug your mum. Just see how you get on. Little things go a long way.

BOOST THEM, BOOST YOURSELF.

As you've probably realised by now, I've written this book to share my view that *everyone* is unique and *everyone* can find something they love. This holds true for sports and physical activities too – if you love sports and being active, then with **hard work** and **resilience**, anyone should be able to play and compete in whatever gets their blood pumping. True, some people might have to open a few more doors or push a bit harder than others, but that shouldn't stop them from **achieving their goals**. It's a message I'm proud to champion, and it's powerfully supported by the incredible feats of human ability we witness during the **Paralympics**.

But can you believe the first official Paralympics was only held in **1960**? While that may seem like a long time ago, consider that it's been more than **2,000 years** since the first Olympic Games!

The idea behind the Paralympics came after World War Two when a guy called Dr Ludwig Guttmann set up a rehabilitation centre for people with spinal injuries at **Stoke Mandeville Hospital** in the UK. He wanted to boost the patients' **happiness** by encouraging them to get **active**. Sound familiar?

Eventually Dr Guttmann's idea grew and, inspired by London's **1948 Olympic Games**, he set up an event where patients could compete for prizes. One thing led to another and in 1952, the **Stoke Mandeville Games** (as they became known) were founded.

These games then morphed into the first ever Paralympic Games in Rome, Italy in 1960. Then in 1976, the first **Winter Paralympics** was held in Sweden. Now we compete in the same cities as the Olympics every four years – which makes sense, because *para* means '**alongside**' in Greek. And guess what? Their popularity just keeps growing and growing.

Now, the Paralympics are more popular than ever! For instance, more than 4.1 billion (yes, **BILLION**) people from all over the world sat down to watch Rio's 2016 Paralympics on TV. That was more people than the Olympics that year, and was 7 per cent more than for London 2012 (told you it was growing!). Showing I'm not making this up, we saw a bigger increase at the **2020 Tokyo Paralympics** with over 4.25 billion people watching globally. This actually set a new record for the event. Let's hope we beat it again in Paris 2024!

FAST FACT:

The first Paralympic Games in 1960 involved 400 athletes from 23 countries. But Tokyo's 2020/2021 Paralympics involved 4,500 athletes from 162 nations!

This growing interest shows that the Paralympics are increasingly being seen as so much more than just a partner for (or something to merely sit 'alongside') the Olympics. They're an **amazing sporting contest** in their own right, with all the highs, lows, thrills and spills of any other sporting contest. Which is no surprise really, as what could be cooler than watching a bunch of tough and talented athletes smash perceptions about what people think they can do – and show off the power of the human body (and mind) in the process?

Athletes with disabilities **push the boundaries** of human potential by achieving **awe-inspiring feats**, from seeing someone with one leg jumping huge heights to watching a blind athlete swimming with precise technique. It's a fiercely competitive environment where medals are won by the **best**, not by the people with the most inspirational story. It's an event that highlights what the human brain and body can achieve, driven by passion, determination **and a whole heap of hard work**.

In the run-up to the London 2012 Paralympics, I was part of an advertising campaign called '**Meet the Superhumans**' that also championed this message. It was a proud moment for me to stand strong with all these other powerful athletes and show people that human beings really are **incredible**. And this is the idea I wanted to get across in this book. That the human body and brain are capable of much more than we think they are, and when they're given the tools to reach their full potential – **amazing** things can happen.   *There's that magic I was talking about again!*

Making Waves

The brilliant Ellie Simmonds was only thirteen when she won not one, but TWO gold medals in swimming at the 2008 Paralympics. Ellie, who has achondroplasia (a type of dwarfism), was a huge influence on me. Starting her career a few years before me, I watched her soar and hoped I could do the same. She was also one of my co-Superhumans in the London 2012 ad campaign as well as a fellow *Strictly* performer! She does so much to raise awareness of amazing causes, like disability, adoption and even coral reef restoration. I feel so privileged to have worked with her on some of those initiatives, including a fitness campaign for kids where we disguised ourselves as PE teachers for a day!

REST STOP

Use your voice!

Just like the rest of you, your voice is unique. So use it! Don't lose it! Use your voice to make a difference.

What are the problems around you that you'd like to fix? Maybe there is no school club for people who like running or drawing? Maybe the food in the canteen isn't healthy enough? Maybe there's no nice bench in your town for someone to sit and take a rest if they it? **What can you do about it?**

You could talk to a teacher – or write a letter to your headteacher, or to your town councillor or even your local MP. You could make a poster about it. You could start a club yourself! All of these things probably sound really daunting, and whatever you decide to do will probably depend on what the nature of the problem actually is. But whatever is bothering you, use your voice. Talk to people and raise awareness. And maybe, just maybe, you'll be the one to make things change.

This is a **perfect time** to turn to your **journal**, and ask yourself these questions: *Did I use what I've learned to help someone else? Did I encourage someone even though I wanted to win? Did something change about the way I feel today? Did the koala outrun me or steal my shoelaces?*

Now, you've learned a lot in this book, right? You're feeling all empowered and boosted (I hope!). And you are probably expecting to nail it when you get cracking with everything you've learned.

But before you get too excited, just remember that **not everyone gets the results they want every time**. The important thing to keep in mind, is that not winning at something doesn't mean that you aren't doing well, or getting better – progress is there, even if you can't always see it. There are **always lessons to be learned**. Come on, you're a kid and your journey has barely started. **LEARNING IS ALL PART OF THE FUN!**

> **"You don't take losses, you take lessons."**
>
> – Marcus Rashford

GIVE BACK TO THE PEOPLE THAT HAVE GIVEN YOU SO MUCH.

Your **race in life** will be so much happier with mates alongside you, who share with you and care for you. Coming to the end of this book is sad for me, because I've loved being able to share all this stuff with you. But even though you've now (nearly) finished this book – you're still only just beginning! And I think you're going to do just fine. Use what you've learned, read it again if you want to – and get to work. **Just never forget this ...**

Happiness Hack

Become someone else's coach

Remember I said sharing is caring? Well, now it's time to put that to the test. I want you to use what you've learned throughout this book to inspire others. To help them grow, learn, reach their goals, spread gratitude and find their happiness. It's like how Laura and I have become your coaches in this book, now I want you to try and be a coach to someone else.

But how? I hear you ask. Well, remember the Race Plan at the end of each chapter? I want you to use the prompts in your Race Plan and share them with someone else. You can do this by sharing a version of the Race Plan from the next page and giving it to a friend. Or, if you're feeling extra generous, you could actually **give** a friend your copy of my book!

Unless you've drawn all over it!

Then, encourage them to fill out their own plan.
Talk through the different parts and help
them find their own answers. It might sound
daunting — but you've got this.

If I can do it, so can you.

Helping someone else discover how to find their
happiness will make you feel amazing. ← Trust me!
And it might help you in the process! Because?
Sharing is caring.

RACE PLAN: *LAP EIGHT*

This is your Race Plan. All eight laps of it! Fill it in or copy it out in your journal and write down your answers. You can also photocopy it or make a version to share with your friends. Pass on the knowledge you've learned to help them succeed!

LAP ONE: Write down three things you like about yourself. Then write down what your teacher, a grown-up in your life and a friend would say are your three strengths:

....

....

....

LAP TWO: Write down five things that bring you joy:

....

....

....

....

....

LAP THREE: Write down your top three goals and how you will celebrate achieving them:

....

....

....

LAP FOUR: Write down three things you're grateful for. Then write down when you plan to practise your 'Three Great Things' exercise so you can try and do it every day:

....

....

....

LAP FIVE: Write down five new things you're going to try. If you can link them to your goals, even better!

....

....

....

....

....

LAP SIX: Write down three mantras or affirmations you will use when something doesn't go your way or you need some calming words. Will you write them down or create a poster using the words to hang on your wall?

....

....

....

LAP SEVEN: Write down three people who are already on your team and one person you'd like on your team:

....

....

....

....

LAP EIGHT: Write down one person you want to share what you've learned with:

....

You can use this space for any notes you want to
make about what you've learnt in this chapter!

THE FINISH LINE

THE FINISH LINE

C'est fini! See? I'm practising my French for Paris 2024.

Ooh la la!

So, we are coming to the end of the race and the **finish line is in sight**. We are moving so fast the crowd is a blur, but I can hear them chanting your name.

I will <u>never ever</u> forget the sound of **80,000 people** in the stadium at London 2012 chanting, '**Peacock! Peacock! Peacock!**' At least, I hope that was what they were saying. There could have been an actual peacock at the starting line with me, along with a **koala** munching away at an Olympic wreath of eucalyptus leaves, a **porpoise** still trying to figure out how to tie its shoes, not to mention all my team members and fabulously talented competitors. They might have all been there. I wasn't looking. I just had my head on the goal.

But honestly, I often think back to how I started my journey – as a **five-year-old boy** so unwell in hospital that the doctors didn't think I would make it.

How I woke up and everything had changed in the blink of an eye. In that moment, the fact that one day I'd be competing in a stadium as a Paralympic athlete seems nothing short of UNBELIEVABLE. But I have so much to thank for how I got there and couldn't be more grateful for the support, luck and hard work that went into that moment because it's led me here. To you!

Now, we've talked about a lot of stuff over the course of this book. We've talked about being different and how that's a good thing – how that makes you unique. And about finding your porpoise – sorry! – your **purpose**, and the things you love doing. We've talked about **challenging yourself** to get out of that comfort zone and do something sca-a-a-ry, something that makes your knees knock and your tummy wobble but that makes you feel GREAT afterwards! (Hello again, serotonin and dopamine!) Then we've talked too about finding and building **your dream team** (all those brilliant people who support you) and about **harnessing their positivity**. AND – most importantly of all – about GIVING SOMETHING BACK. About **passing on all that knowledge** to someone else. Someone else who needs help finding what it is they love.

Phew! There is a lot there to get your head around, and you might want to go back over a few bits. That's completely fine – in fact, it's a great idea to help keep it all fresh in your mind. And don't forget your **Race Plan**! Those excellent sections at the end of each chapter that you filled out will help to **motivate** you as you continue your journey – so HANG ON TO THEM!

I'm not suggesting for a moment that you need to become an elite athlete or sportsperson or anything like that. **You just need to find what makes YOU happy**. And you can use the skills you've gained from this book to do that AND to keep growing and learning to accomplish whatever **goals** you set yourself. Do you remember right back at the beginning when I said this book is about **being the best and happiest version of yourself**? Well, THAT'S the version of yourself that you should **always** try to be. Not just when you're doing an activity, but in everything you do – that's the **you** you want to be when you're at school, when you meet your friends or take an exam, or EVEN when you get a job! Yes, that distant day waaaaay in the future, when you have to

be a RESPONSIBLE ADULT! ⟵ Scary!

Even then you can use the things you've learned in these pages. Because you'll still be the same person when you're grown up – you'll still be you. Just like I'm still me.

But listen, I've been lucky. I didn't get to where I am because I'm special. I got there because I had **support,** because those supportive people **helped me find my dream**, and because **I DIDN'T GIVE UP FIGHTING TO GET THERE**. And that's what I want for **you**. I want you to find in here the support you need to take the first (and maybe second or third!) step on your journey to finding your dreams, so you too can reach the **potential that is already in you**.

YOU CAN DO ANYTHING. It says so on the front of this book, and I hope I've given you the ideas, inspiration and tools to make it all happen for you. It might be a sprint, it might be a marathon, but either way, **you've got this**.

I hope you keep this book (especially if you've written in it or unless you've given it to a friend) so you can look back when you need a bit of a boost, or a leg-up (ha ha). You **REALLY DO** have the skills inside you to smash everything.

Hopefully you will sprint to your goals alongside good friends and family who believe in you, and you will be grateful and happy along the way. **That is a lot to achieve in 10 seconds**! It does take work, but it is **so worth doing**. WHO DOESN'T WANT TO BE THE BEST PERSON THEY CAN BE?

I will keep cheering for you, and I hope you will do the same for me.

Love,
Jonnie

A note from Laura Earnshaw:

Wow! Congratulations on reaching the end of this book. I hope you've loved reading it and working through all the exercises as much as I loved collaborating with Jonnie on them! Remember, every day is an opportunity to learn, grow and keep working towards being your very best and finding what makes you happy. As you keep exploring the world and learning about what you love, remember that if something doesn't quite go your way, you can just try again. YOU are amazing. Keep being YOU, and never forget there is only one of you in the whole world, which makes you so special!

Laura

Extra Activities

When the world gets too much and you need to quieten your brain, here are a few tried and tested techniques to help calm you down or get off to sleep.

Grounding exercises

More genius ideas from Laura!

5-4-3-2-1: This is a sensory-based exercise. Take five deep breaths, then name five things you can see, four things you can touch, three things you can hear, two things you can smell and one thing you can taste.

Belly breathing: Lie down and place a small object on your belly. Take twenty slow, deep breaths and watch how the object rises and falls with each breath.

Nature sounds: If you can, go outside in your garden or just any safe outside space. Pay attention to your surroundings, such as birds chirping, the breeze on your skin or the colours around you. Even just three to five minutes in nature can relax us.

Cloud gazing: Find a comfortable spot to lie outdoors and look at the sky or find a cosy spot next to a window. Watch the shapes of the clouds passing by. What shapes can you see? What do you notice about how the clouds are moving? What do you notice about how this makes you feel?

Sleep exercises

Cognitive shuffling: Think of random objects that have no link to one another, for example: rabbit, curtain, light, orange, glass. Doing this mimics the process your brain goes through when you are falling asleep and lets your brain and body know that it is safe to let sleep win.

Progressive muscle relaxation: Lie down and close your eyes. Take slow, deep breaths and start to focus on your feet, legs or toes. Tense your muscles, screwing up your toes if you can. Hold this for ten seconds and then relax. Repeat this on different body parts, moving up from your calves to your thighs, bottom, stomach, chest, arms etc. When finished, your body should feel heavy, relaxed and ready to snooze.

Open and closed: Close your eyes and count to thirty, then open them a slither and count to five. Close your eyes again and count to thirty. Open your eyes a slither and count to five. Close your eyes and take slow, deep breaths through your nose. Repeat until you're fast asleep.

A walk in the woods: Close your eyes and imagine you're walking along a woodland path. Hear birds chirping, twigs crunching and the rustle of leaves in the wind. Find a spot to lie down, a patch of luscious grass next to a sun-bathed brook. Listen to your surroundings and let them relax you all the way to sleep.

ABOUT THE CREATORS (AKA MY BOOK TEAM!)

These are just SOME of the incredible people on my book team, but there are loads more we don't have space to add. You'd be amazed at how many people go into making a book!

Do I really need to introduce myself again? OK, I'm **Jonnie Peacock**. I hope you know that by now. I'm a Paralympic 100-metre sprint champion. I won gold and set the Paralympic record at the age of just 19 at the London 2012 Olympic Games, going on to win gold again, and smash my own record at the Rio Paralympics in 2016. I was the first disabled contestant to compete on the main *Strictly Come Dancing* show and I'm passionate about challenging and changing other people's perceptions around disability.

At the time of writing this book I'm training for the 2024 Paralympics in Paris. But when I'm not training? I love playing video games, eating peri-peri chicken and hanging out with my girlfriend, Sally, and my dogs, Bella and Luna.

By the time you read this book, you might even know how I did!

Laura Earnshaw is the founder of an NHS-backed organisation called myHappymind. MyHappymind are experts in the science behind happiness and help hundreds of thousands of children in schools worldwide develop healthy habits so they can thrive! She lives with her husband, two kids and a lovely Maltipoo called Max in Cheshire. She is also the bestselling author of her own book, *My Happy Mind,* and sits on the board of the world's leading mental health charity, The Mental Health Foundation. When she's not working, she loves long country walks, scuba diving and travelling!

Ashwin Chacko is a positively playful award-winning author, illustrator and motivational speaker. He specialises in joy-filled visual storytelling to bring happiness and encouragement to his work. His mission is to champion creativity and empower people to find their inner spark through his art, books, talks and workshops. He lives with his wife and three kids in Ireland. When he is not working he enjoys exploring the great outdoors with his kids, skateboarding, rock climbing and doing lots and lots of drawing.

Laura Buller is a freelance author and editor who loves nothing more than writing happy, fun, silly and brilliant books for young readers. Which is lucky, because she's been doing it for over 30 years! Originally from America, she currently lives in London with her rock star husband and son, with daughter nearby. In her free time she loves scouring the local charity shops for unique treasures, hitting the beach or tending to her collection of mirror balls.

GLOSSARY

amputate – removing a limb for a medical reason

amputee – person who has had a limb removed

anxiety – extreme feelings of worry and fear

authentic – being unique and genuine

autopilot – being able to do things automatically without thinking

disabled – having a long-term physical and/or mental condition that makes it more difficult to do certain things or access experiences in the same way as non-disabled people

disqualified – not allowed to compete or removed from competing for breaking the rules

dopamine – chemical that gives you feelings of satisfaction and motivation

endorphins – chemicals released when you do something fun, known to lower stress and improve mood

hamstring tendinopathy – painful inflammation in the tendons at the back of your thigh

MBE – British honour awarded by the King or Queen for a particular achievement

meningitis – infection of the lining (or 'membrane') around your brain and spinal cord

neurotransmitter – chemicals that allow neurons to communicate

physiotherapist – someone who can treat disease and injuries

prosthetics – human-made body part to replace limbs

serotonin – neurotransmitter that regulates your mood, sleep and other body functions

synapses – the point where neurons connect and pass electric signals to one another

track and field – athletic competitions involving jumping, running and throwing

T42-44 – as of 2018, a type of track or field event for athletes who have lower limb impairments, but do not use prostheses

T61-64 – as of 2018, a type of track or field event for athletes who run or jump with lower prosthetic limbs

THANK YOUS

A monstrous thank you to the countless people who have made this book possible. It has been amazing to see the incredible effort, talent and time given to help bring these ideas to life and become reality.

To my entire family, girlfriend, friends, coaches and training partners that I've been lucky enough to share this journey with and learn from. To the immense work put in by the two incredible Lauras and Ashwin, and by Emily Ball, Katie Knutton, Lara Hancock, Emma Hobson and the entire team at Bloomsbury. You've all helped shaped this into what it is and I couldn't be more grateful.

And finally, a huge thanks to my agents, Lydia Silver and Andy Digweed, without whom this book would never have got off the starting blocks!

Every single one of you has helped make this book what it is and I owe a huge thank you to all of you – this is our book and I'm so grateful and proud of every one of you. Thank you.

ONE LAST THING ...

Did you think I'd forgotten about that?

Remember on page 9 I asked you to write down how you felt before starting this book? Well, turns out I've got one last thing for you to do before you close this book and get back to whatever it was you were doing before. I want you to write down how you feel NOW. Now that you've finished the entire book. All 240 pages of it.

I feel ....

Take a look at what you wrote down at the start. How does it compare? What do you notice?

I really hope you've written a positive word – happy, calm, inspired – but if not, try to remember all you have to do is keep trying to work out what brings you joy, keep working at that mind-body connection and keep trying to figure out who you are. You can't be happy all the time, but you can find what makes you smile.

Like I say, you can do anything. You've got this!
Love,
Jonnie x